WALKING THE WALL

The story in words and pictures of a coast-to-coast walk along Hadrian's Wall

—— TONY HOPKINS ——

KEEPDATE PUBLISHING
Newcastle upon Tyne

Published by Keepdate (Publishing) Ltd
21 Portland Terrace, Jesmond,
Newcastle upon Tyne NE2 1QQ

Copyright © Tony Hopkins

First edition 1993

ISBN 0-9520494-0-6

Apart from any fair dealing for the purposes of research or private study, or criticism or review, as permitted under the Copyright, Designs and Patents Act 1988, this publication may be reproduced, stored or transmitted, in any forms or by any means, only with the prior permission in writing of the publishers, or in the case of reprographic reproduction in accordance with the terms of licences issued by the Copyright Licensing Agency. Inquiries concerning reproduction outside those terms should be sent to the publishers at the address above.

Typeset and designed by Keepdate Ltd, Newcastle upon Tyne
Printed and bound by Butler & Tanner, Ltd, Somerset.

CONTENTS

Page

Chapter 1 *South Shields - Newcastle* 1

Chapter 2 *Newcastle - Harlow Hill* 19

Chapter 3 *Harlow Hill - Chollerford* 43

Chapter 4 *Chollerford - Haughton Common* 59

Chapter 5 *Haughton Common - Greenhead* 77

Chapter 6 *Greenhead - Carlisle* 101

Chapter 7 *Carlisle - Bowness* 121

Further Information 143

Index 145

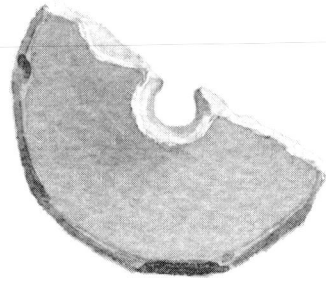

For Andrew And Neal

Introduction

Hadrian's Wall set the bounds to an empire, and its dramatic ruins now provide a theme for thousands of coast to coast walkers. But Roman remains are only part of the story. People visiting the Wall are soon impressed by the quality of the landscape, the variety of the fauna and flora, and the mix of history and prehistory. It is a unique place and casts a powerful spell.

This is the story of a week's walk from the east coast to the west, along the Wall or through adjacent countryside. Most of the pictures were painted on the spot or from life, and the text has been expanded from notes taken along the way. Background information has been woven into every page, so that the book can be used as a source of ideas and explanations, to whet the appetite or spur memories. Above all, this book is about the spirit of a special place.

There is no single way to explore the Wall, though work is continuing to establish a National Trail which will one day take its place in the repertoire of classic long distance walks. At present, and for a few years to come, people will have to find their own route and make their own choices.

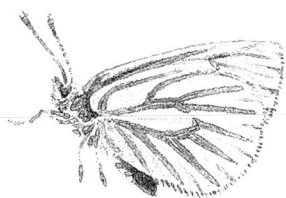

1 South Shields - Newcastle

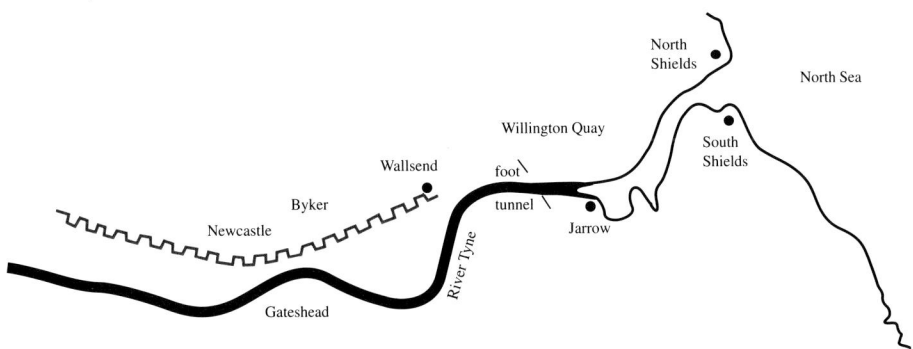

South Shields - Newcastle: 11 miles

Far out to sea a small boat was ploughing into the wind. Lines of gannets crossed its bows, returning from fishing flights far to the south. From the heel of the pier it was hard to make out the horizon. The gannets wove a silver thread between sea and sky, and the shadows of the swell melted into the clouds.

Below the pier, herring gulls and kittiwakes wheeled in the updraught of air, flexing their wings. Tradition among the North Sea fleets has it that gulls are the souls of dead seamen and kittiwakes are drowned children. The cliffs and stacks towards Marsden were white with these ghostly seabirds roosting at their nests; every few minutes a swirl of sound reached out across the water as parties of them gathered and left to search for shoals of herring and sandeels.

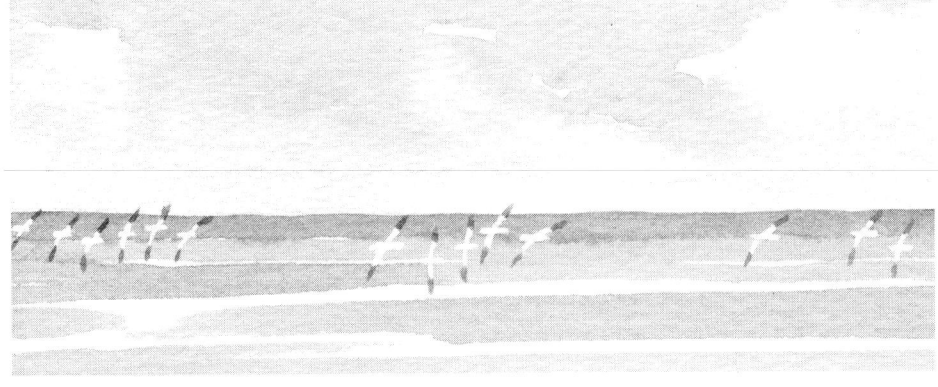

Kittiwakes

The town of South Shields owes its existence to the sea, but it no longer sets its clock by the tide. In the pale early morning light, it was still sleeping. Nothing stirred along Harbour Drive; the tourist car parks were empty, no-one had yet set foot on Littlehaven Beach.

The mouth of the Tyne narrows between two promontories, North and South Shields. 'Shield' means a temporary summer settlement, which may have been all there was for centuries. The burgesses of Newcastle petitioned the King in the early fourteenth century to prevent the rivermouth sites from competing against the powerful city for trade, and until Victorian times the suppression worked.

South Shields survived on a varied diet of chemical and salt-works, smelting and glass-making, until Newcastle burst at the seams and heavy industry, ship-building and coal-handling flooded downstream and immersed the town.

But many centuries before, the promontory of Lawe Top housed people of the Iron Age, and it was to here that the Romans came in 80 AD, to establish an expeditionary force and supply base. Watching the little fishing boat as it nosed between the beacons of the piers and found the safety it was seeking in Shields Harbour, it took no great flight of imagination to see the Tyne as the perfect anchorage for Agricola's fleet, or Shields Lawe as the obvious site for a fort.

Littlehaven Beach lies at the lower arc of the Tyne entrance, bounded on one side by the South Pier and on the other by the South Groyne, the lip or spur at the mouth of the river. Making the first footprints across it after the falling tide was like whispering in a cathedral. At the far side stood the Groyne Lighthouse - an iron beacon, rust-red and topped by a black-backed gull. Close by was a new housing development and the fenced yard of the sailing club, and beside this an unclaimed wilderness where the eddy of the tide behind the groyne had dumped a shelf of wrack.

A cobbled patio of city flotsam - beautifully weathered house-bricks and plastic bottles - led up to the high tide mark. Between this and the road verge was a twist of marram grass and a slack or dell a few feet across where laburnum and willow shrubs had defied developers. A tiny bird had taken refuge and was trying to hide among the foliage, slipping into shadows and dropping from leaf to leaf so that it was impossible to get a clear view.

This skulking behaviour in birds sets the pulse of bird-watchers racing; in the autumn, migrant warblers from Siberia or Scandinavia often overshoot on their way south and end up in places along the East Coast. Such unlikely sanctuary must have saved many vagrants. This bird looked like a willow warbler, the commonest of the 'leaf' warblers. Even though it was June it seemed tired, hungry and reluctant to fly, as if it had made landfall only hours before.

Across the river lay Tynemouth Priory, the lifeboat station and the Fish Quay. The town was beginning to wake up; smoke was rising from chimneys and the fish market was busy. Back along Harbour Drive a runner glided along

South Pier from Seahaven Beach, South Shields. Sun rising behind the bank of clouds.

the pavement, past beds of grey poplar and sea buckthorn. Other footprints now appeared on the beach. Back at the South Pier the Customs Office was opening. The red-brick building of the Port of Tyne Authority boasted the loud paintwork of marigold and blue, typically bright colours of a seaside town.

Beyond the South Pier was Seahaven Beach, leading to Trow Point and Frenchman's Bay, a fine sweep of sand backed by the grassy Leas. At one time, this was an industrial landscape, littered with colliery waste and carrying the line of the 'Marsden Rattler'. South Shields was famous for the Three Collieries of Harton, Hilda and Westoe, but it is also a town of public parks, and the local Corporation bought the Leas to keep them green.

Two distant figures were moving slowly along the beach, bearing black plastic sacks and picking up litter as they went. They picked up everything - oiled pebbles, tins, clusters of whelk eggs, all the treasures of a seaside adventure. The beach was clean after they had passed. No possibility of finding a Roman coin or a shard of pottery.

A last look at the sea revealed it had turned ash blue as the sun climbed out of the cloud. The horizon was now clear; gannets still swept up the coast to Bass Rock, and the disembodied bridge of a coaster shimmered above the swell.

A line of gannets heading north, towards the famous breeding site at Bass Rock.

Sea Road, leading into Ocean Road, lies at the heart of the Victorian seaside resort that formed present-day South Shields. The South and North Marine Parks were created late last century from the mountains of salt waste and ballast sand that had been dumped about the town.

Close to the Pier Parade and Pavilion is a clocktower celebrating Victoria's jubilee in 1887, and commemorating the invention of the self-righting lifeboat. The need for a lifeboat had become undeniable in 1789, when the town witnessed the loss of the *'Adventure'* just 300 yards off shore. A prize was offered for the best design and this was won by Henry Greathead, but several essential and innovative features (notably the self-righting device) were  borrowed from the plans of another contestant called William Wouldhave. Although both are now credited with the invention it was Greathead who won the prize, took the contract to build the boat, and received a handsome reward from the government.

Present-day Ocean Road was full of fish and chip shops and Tandoori takeaways. Turning right and climbing Lawe Road however, the Roman influence soon became obvious; the side-streets are named after emperors Vespasian and Trajan and there was a replica standard at the entrance to the park at the top of the hill. In the park, children exercised remote control cars and a group of council workmen played golf in their blue overalls.

The Lawe must have been the obvious place for the Romans to build a fort, a defensible island overlooking the rivermouth. But it was hard at first to see through the brightly-painted houses to a time when there was nothing here but a military installation. To the local population of Brigantian farmers, the Roman fort must have generated the same sort of terror as a Soviet missile base in the 1960s.

Past the People's Mission and the old Infants' School, occupying a green field surrounded by terraced streets, lay the ruins of Arbeia. It looked unimpressive. The fort had been built and rebuilt, the headquarters facing one way and then the other, and the rubble marking out the barracks and granaries crisscrossed in confusion. But then, by way of total contrast, there loomed the reconstructed West Gate. It was big, cold and immaculate; two impregnable towers and enough of the wall to lodge forcefully in the imagination. This brought Hadrian's Wall to life in a way that no text-book possibly could.

From the walkway above the gates, having climbed tower stairs and peered through the windows, there were wide views to the west. The course of the river could be picked out in ship-yards and the cranes of the Swan Hunter Yard marked where Hadrian's Wall began.

Arbeia was built by the Sixth Legion in Hadrian's days as part of the Wall system. Presumably there was no need to continue the curtain-wall this far, but there may have been towers or fortlets acting as links in a chain towards Wallsend, although no ruins have been found. Arbeia's prime was around 210 AD when the Emperor Severus led campaigns into Scotland and made the fort his supply base. It was the storage area for all the army's grain and gear.

The well at Arbeia Roman Fort, South Shields.

Not much remains to tell the tale. Most of the usable stone was taken away centuries ago to make farmhouses and churches; the residue simply marks out the skeletons of where things were. On this morning, some volunteers were barrowing soil from a new area of excavation at the south east corner, and they told tales of the Commanding Officer's House, of an ornamental pond and a gold ring embedded in a wall. Some of the recent finds were on show in the little museum. But the lasting memory of Arbeia was the gate, re-built in 1988.

Across the road, on the patch of grass that hides Arbeia's vicus or civilian settlement, a group of boys were playing football. The river was nearby, reached by steps from the Turk's Head and crossing River Drive to Wapping Street. A patch of open ground destined to be part of the Seamanship and Survival Centre was where the Roman port may have been. Clumps of mallow and Oxford ragwort - cosmopolitan weeds of every city from here to Rome - cast a veil over the broken ground.

Oxford ragwort, a flower of waste ground and crevices in old walls and pavements.

In the days of sail and steam, Wapping Street was where the old sea captains lived. Tarred huts now house the South Tyneside College Boatyard and the Merchant Navy Fire Training Centre. An alley between the buildings led to a wharf, next to Forsyth's Fish Merchant and the Gambling Man Gallery. Smoke wreathed the Fire Training Centre, and beside a blackened boiler door a team of trainees were trying to clean the soot off their faces. Offshore, a flotilla of small boats, *Osprey, Neptune* and *Guiding Star*, bobbed and curtsied and tugged at their moorings.

A new footpath led south with the curve of the river to a viewpoint overlooking the derelict Graving Dock and its rail terminal, a dead-and-alive corner due to be conserved and embraced as part of the Shields story. Downstream, the Market Place Ferry had left its landing stage and was on its way across the river to North Shields, bearing shoppers. The yellow *Shieldsman* ferry replaced the 'black, dumpy, smoke-belching' version which ended its days when the terminal was wrecked in 1970. Two hundred years ago wherries did the same job, more gracefully, but taking anything up to three hours against the tide.

Walking south and keeping faith with the river, along Ferry Street and past The Alum House Inn, down Mill Dam to the Corporation Quay and the restored Corn Mill, it became obvious that seafaring has soaked into every fibre of South Shields, and that the accompanying trade had been both its salvation and downfall, when the industry collapsed.

Two small boys were fishing from the quay opposite the old Customs House. They knew every eddy and swell of the river and could have belonged to another century; their talk was of 'sprats and flatties' and they wore dusty corduroys and patched shirts.

Corporation Street carried on southwards, past the Tyne Docks where four great timber staithes had once borne the coal brought by rail from the pits in the region, to ships which served a hundred ports and kept industry alive all over Europe. It was the coal-laden colliers that attracted both French privateers in the Napoleonic Wars and German U-boats in the Second World War.

A stiff breeze whipped up dust and shreds of litter from the road, past a timber yard and a new housing estate bearing a plaque commemorating the site of William Black Street, where Catherine Cookson grew up. The road was fast, noisy and a bit bleak.

Roads and roundabouts, and miles of robust and alien shrubs, are characteristic of much of South Tyneside. Many of the schemes for improvement and slum clearance were the brainchild of John Reid, the Borough Engineer in the formative years before and after the Second World War. His nick-name was 'Road Island Reid', a wry comment from people who knew more about chickens than traffic flows.

Most of what was once East Jarrow has now gone. To the left of the dual carriageway is the Mitsumi UK factory, with some timber yards on the right, but just beyond that nothing is visible except the Alkali Inn. There was an Alkali factory nearby, which made epsom salts and sulphuric acid, but both the factory and its associated community were dismantled years ago and the inn now stands in splendid isolation.

A cold wind blew over Jarrow Slake. Having to peer through hoardings and concrete fences, across stacks of timber and piles of rubble, took away any lingering vision of this wasteland as an inter-tidal mudflat. It was reclaimed for industrial use in the early 1970s. For a century before that it had been used to lay out and season timber, which accounts for the numerous timber merchants in the area.

Redshank running over the open mud.

Mudflat and salting are rich in wildlife, but their beauty is in the soul of whoever has the time to sit and watch. Jarrow had to earn a living from ship-building and mining and the Slake had few friends.

The Slake is also the setting for a well-told tale. In 1832 a miner from the Alfred Pit was accused of murdering a magistrate near to the Slake. There was a strike on and the community was being starved into submission. Miners William Jobling and Ralph Armstrong were drunk as well as hungry and stopped the magistrate at the toll-gate to beg money. Armstrong dragged the man from his horse and beat him. The old magistrate lived long enough to clear Jobling of the attack but he was the only man caught. He was hanged, tarred and gibbeted. His body was left out in an iron cage overlooking the Slake - a monument to as much justice as many pitmen thought they ever received.

On the far west side of the waste stood the crouched figure of St Paul's Church. A right turn off the A185, past another timber yard, led to the little churchyard on the shoulder of the river Don. With the tide out, the river had dwindled to nothing. Outside, St Paul's was no more than a blackened church and a few ruins eaten by acid rain. Inside, it was an Anglo-Saxon time machine and home of the Venerable Bede. It is a paradox that Northumbria's greatest jewels only survived because they were lost in godless places. Escomb, in the middle of a council estate in County Durham, is the most beautiful Anglo-Saxon church in Britain. St Paul's and St Peter's, a few miles away at Monkwearmouth, are the pivot around which culture and art radiated across northern Europe.

Bede was an historian and writer who set down only what he was sure was the truth. This made him unique among his peers, and his *History of the English Church and People* is one of the few reliable records of what happened in Britain from Roman to Saxon times.

Bede spent the whole of his adult life at Jarrow. All his knowledge was gleaned from books, brought back to the monasteries of St Peter's and St Paul's by more adventurous monks, notably Benedict Biscop who travelled to Rome several times and established St Peter's in 674 AD. St Paul's at Jarrow followed in 681. The two monasteries, or 'one monastery with two houses', flourished only until the Viking raids of 794, but by then the die was cast. Biscop had introduced crafts from south-east Europe. Ecclesiastical buildings were thereafter made from stone, elaborately decorated. The insular Celtic traditions were overturned and after the Synod of Whitby the Church looked increasingly to Rome.

Several of the internal features of St Paul's echoed what must have been a spiritual revolution. The walls of the chancel, the original eighth century church, were tall and smooth with small windows and some of the original

St Paul's Church at Jarrow, from the south-east. The chancel is Saxon and the tower Norman. Stonework blackened by the industrial revolution.

The blocked-in north door of the chancel. The stones were cut by Roman masons and re-used by Saxons.

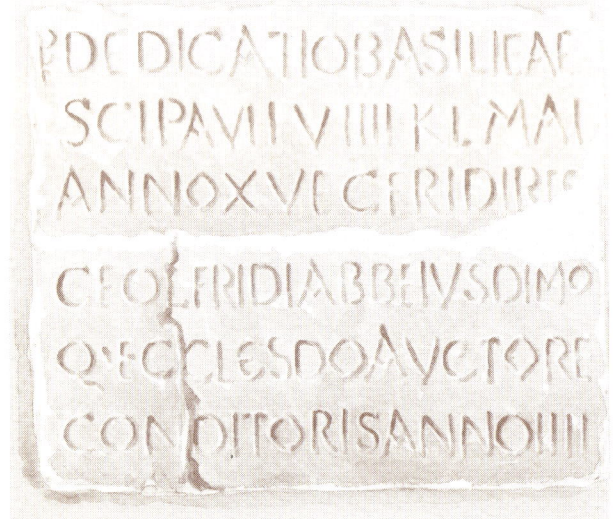

The dedication stone, set above the chancel arch.
'The dedication of the church of St Paul's on the ninth of Kalends of May in the fifteenth year of King Ecgfrith and the fourth year of Ceolfrith, abbot, and with God's help the founder of this church.'

Three beautifully carved fragments of stonework, lying on the floor of the north aisle at St Paul's. Vine scrolls with wood pigeons, squirrels and a hunter and serpent.

stained glass. An inscribed stone gave the date of dedication as the fifteenth year of King Ecgfrith and the fourth year of the Abbot Ceolfrith. Close to a blocked-in doorway on the north wall was a battered oak seat that looked as if it had been used by every scholar since Bede and is reputed to have been his chair. It looked suitably uncomfortable - low and narrow with a tall straight back and medieval graffiti.

Stones stacked in the shadows of the north aisle included baluster shafts and other worthy pieces of masonry from the Saxon church. Had they been displayed in cases they would have appeared as no more than the dust of history, but because they were strewn along the floor they radiated some of the life that had gone into making them.

Three fragments in particular were eye-catching; they had obviously come from a screen or frieze and were covered in elaborate scrolls of foliage. Among the swirling vine stems on one of the fragments was a pair of wood pigeons, on another a pair of squirrels, and on the third a human figure, a hunter or falconer, facing a serpent. Whoever had carved them had fused Celtic and Mediterranean styles and knew the ways of wild birds and animals. Such skill in the early eighth century must have been rare and highly prized. Perhaps Benedict Biscop's masons went on from here to create the Ruthwell and Bewcastle crosses, and to teach local apprentices who then continued the tradition down the years to create the Chapter Houses at Southwell and York.

Outside, the stonework of the Saxon and Norman monastery had suffered from a century of polluted air and was black and corroded. Even so, it was easy to see that most of it had come from Arbeia or even Hadrian's Wall, and owed its facing-work to Roman masons. Until the last century no-one would have thought twice about robbing ancient monuments of building stone.

On the wall of the refectory, at head-height and obvious against the black stone, sat a puss moth. Her furry white coat was evolved for camouflage and she looked spectacularly out of place. As a caterpillar she must have grown

Female puss moth.

up on the poplar trees overlooking the church gate, and pupated on their bark. Puss moths have adapted well to town life and are found wherever there are sallows and poplars. For such big creatures the adult moths are not often seen; they spend the day tucked up asleep, usually on tree trunks.

The Don runs north to the Tyne, below the monastery ruins. Reclamation work and tree-planting had been carried out all along the muddy channel, but the view of the Slake from the track was still barren. At the outfall of the Don there was a jetty; the grassy riverbank, known as Quay Corner, served as a picnic spot for the families of shipyard workers at the turn of the century. In the Great War the view of the Tyne would have been dominated by the Palmer Yard and its battleships. A Zeppelin attack in 1915 failed to do very much damage to the place but the Depression of the early 1930s destroyed it completely.

Below the timbers of the jetty was a bank of silt, all that was left of the real Jarrow Slake. An oystercatcher stood sleeping out on the glistening dog-tooth of mud, head to the wind, rocking on one leg, waiting for the falling tide to call it back to the estuary.

Having seen so little open country along the south bank of the Tyne it was easy to lose touch with the fauna and flora of the river. The carvings in the church had struck the point home by showing how ancestors had blended nature with art to lift the spirit of the age. But that had happened in a cloister. The church had been no more than a pebble on the beach; currents had washed around it and left the flotsam of more trying times.

The call of a redshank suddenly shattered the quietness. It was just a few feet away. The triple echo, *tieu-hu-hu*, rolled across the Slake. Waders have fluting calls evolved to carry over miles of saltings. The North-East coast is a winter home for thousands, but only several hundred stay to breed. Redshanks are noisy and nervous sentinels of the marshes, fewer in number as there are fewer empty places along the river. It was surprising to find one here, yet considering all the wasteland on either side of the Don it shouldn't have been.

Redshank, the warden of the marshes. Noisy and nervous, feathers held flat.

Nesting redshanks are always watchful and this particular bird had chosen the highest vantage point possible, on top of a telegraph pole. It obviously had a nest or family in the tussocks of grass over the bank to the west, and was being as belligerent as it dared. Backtracking to avoid the confrontation succeeded in attracting the attention of a lapwing which also had a nest to guard. The only escape was to make a quick dash to Curlew Road, a narrow track flanked by tall concrete fences and piles of rubble. This looked safe but after a few yards there was a soft flurry of tawny wings as a wall brown butterfly launched itself from a dust-heap and made what amounted to a threatening gesture. Even butterflies can be territorial.

Somewhere near here, on high ground overlooking the river, the Romans may have built a fort. The only evidence is documentary, from a listing in the Notitia by which the Romans recorded the Wall garrisons. Only the name, Danum, survives.

Two youths were running a lurcher on the bare ground towards a row of oil tanks. Like many people in Jarrow they were angry about the state of the Slake. There is a current plan to dredge it and make a dock for building oil rigs, but as they spoke they shook their heads and smiled in disbelief. The lurcher cocked its leg against the concrete fence and went off to look for rats.

Further on, the Gaslight Inn was silent and the streets empty. Hidden underfoot was the Tyne Tunnel, carrying a stream of traffic from East Jarrow to Willington and Howdon. Closer to the river was the entrance to the pedestrian and cyclists' tunnel, the forgotten way across the river. The escalator hummed, the cream and green tiles echoed; there is a deafening quiet about the journey beneath the Tyne. The pedestrian tunnel was opened in 1951, sixteen years before the vehicle link. In its heyday it was used by thousands of shipyard workers, but times have changed; most who still have jobs now have cars.

The escalator was eerie. Although obviously designed to London Underground plans there was no dirt, no advertising, no graffiti, no commuters and no trains. Half way across there was a line showing where Durham and Northumberland once met.

On the other side North Tyneside was bathed in bright sunshine. After the soft cream light of the tunnel the open air was hard and cobalt. To the left stood the Antimony Works of the Cookson Mineral Co. Everything looked clean and new; there was no breath of history about the place and it was a surprise to discover that George Stephenson had lived in a little cottage on the site in 1802.

Left along Hadrian Road, past Willington Quay, heavy industry crowded the river. The scale of sheet metal and marine engineering works was daunting; everything seemed to have been built by giants. At the Hadrian Yard there was a gap of wasteland, earmarked for building, with a clear view of the river. An oil platform was in the late stages of construction, a glittering monster wrapped in scaffolding, all its lines and angles picked out by strings of lights. It was alive; it grew, breathed and moved. Men were working on the decks in clusters like blackfly on the petals of a great steel rose.

The road crossed Willington Gut, a broad drain rather than a river, then passed Point Pleasant alongside the Metro viaduct and embankment. Gorse and willow brightened the banks. Hadrian Road Metro Station, then the Hadrian Park pub, made it obvious that the Wall was close.

The cranes of Swan Hunter are the most imposing skyline feature of the river. They too looked as if they had been built by giants. They brooded over Wallsend, squinting down their long noses at the failing shipyards. Just after the main yard entrance, marked by an ornate blue clock-tower, Hadrian Road turned into Buddle Lane and crossed a green square. Here was the site of Segedunum, the Roman fort at the end of the Wall.

Wallsend. The cranes of Swan Hunter and the grassed over remains of Segedunum Roman Fort.

It seemed a great pity that someone had gone to the trouble of exposing the foundations of the fort and laying out a lawn. It would have been much better to have pretended it wasn't there. The base of the headquarters building was jailed behind high railings, and the outer walls were marked in concrete. There wasn't enough visible to appreciate how the fort would have looked, but too much to leave things to the imagination.

Segedunum fort, and the stretch of Wall to Newcastle, was an afterthought by the Romans; it wasn't part of Hadrian's plan. There must have been good reasons for worrying about the lack of defences along this stretch of the river, probably something to do with attacks from raiders crossing at low tide. So when the whole strategy of the Wall system was reviewed in its early years (around 130 AD) the chance was taken to extend it and build the fort. The site was well-chosen, on a platform over an angle of the river, with a clear view down the Long Reach towards South Shields. From the east corner-tower a short stretch of Wall ran down into the river, but the remains were removed by Swan Hunter to make way for the SS Mauritania. Other fragments have suffered a similar fate, or been buried.

Wallsend was a pit village in the early nineteenth century, and any Roman stones that came to hand were used in colliery buildings. In 1884 new streets were set out and built over the old pit, and now these in turn have been demolished. The land has a story to tell but many of the ghosts have fled.

Below the four-acre rectangle of the fort lay an old railway line, due to become a cycleway and part of the National Trail. This runs south and west to Walker and Byker and might have made a better walk, but a look at the map confirmed that the quicker route, and the line of the Wall, kept to the main road.

It was late afternoon. Neptune Road turned into Fossway, the long straight road towards Newcastle. In the last century birch woodland covered most of the area and the Wall stood four feet tall, but no trace remains. Past Brough Park and the turquoise-painted works of NEI Parsons, then onto Shields Road, there was little to linger over. The Byker Wall, the mile-long block of tenements to the south of the road, was in shadow, looking like a mediaeval cliff-settlement of troglodytes.

Once over Byker Bridge there was a choice of making for the Tyne or following New Bridge Street into the city centre. Swirls of gulls over the quayside decided the matter. Turning left down Gibson Street led to City Road and the edge of the old town. On the right was the Keelman's Hospital, a tall fine-featured building within sight and sound of the river. Keels were the shallow-draughted boats that carried coal out from the staithes to the colliers; the hospital was built in 1701 by the keelmen for their poor and needy. Its central tower bore a clock and a square sundial, each telling a different time.

Rowan and rose trees, cotoneaster and periwinkle covered the verge beside the Barley Mow pub. A flight of steps led down towards the river. On the west side of the road, quayside redevelopment was in full swing behind the Law Court and Sallyport Crescent (Sallyport was one of the Town Gates, from where the garrison sallied forth). There was a freshly opened vista to the west, culminating in All Saints Church which lies on the line of Hadrian's Wall. At the bottom of the steps was Sandgate, ancestral home of the keelmen and named after another gate in the Town Walls.

A roadside rose-bush near Byker Bridge.

The river made and shaped Newcastle. The Romans brought their vessels upstream, created a fort and a settlement, a bridge to carry the road to the North, and a Wall to mark the limit of the Empire. When the Empire crumbled the river still flowed, bringing trade and wealth to merchants and burgesses. The 'New Castle' was built by the Normans in the eleventh century and replaced with the Castle Keep in the twelfth century. The Town Walls of the thirteenth century protected the burgesses and their wealth from the Scots. The thread through history was the river.

Upstream the evening sky was shot with colours, cyanine to apricot. Silhouetted against this were six bridges, the motif of the modern city. Downstream was the Baltic Flour Mill, a fitting epitaph to an age of merchant venturers. Around it and across the Tyne, gulls wheeled and turned.

Kittiwakes, and perhaps the souls of the dead, danced in the dusk.

2 Newcastle - Harlow Hill

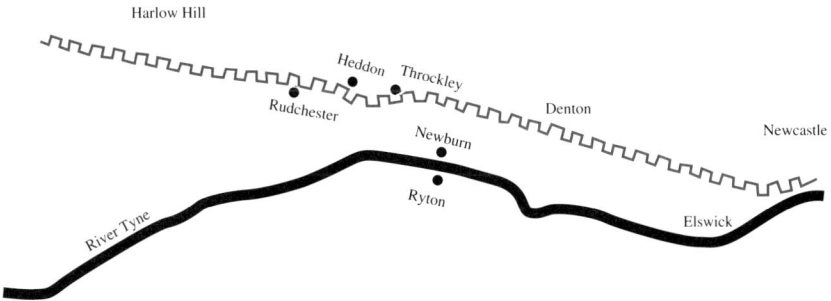

Newcastle - Harlow Hill: 13 miles

Sparks of blue light winked across shop windows as an ambulance took the corner into Percy Street and headed up towards the Haymarket. Eldon Square pigeons shuffled about on sills and gables, only half inclined to fly.

The stillness of the early morning closed in around St Andrew's Church. There was no breath of wind to stir the accumulated litter of Gallowgate. The air, the pigeons and the city traders were all gathering for the day. With the football season over, St James' Park looked forlorn.

The best glimpse into Newcastle's history comes with the West Walls, across the road between the bus station and Stowell Street. The Town Walls were built in the thirteenth and fourteenth centuries; the longest surviving section, running behind Stowell Street, was finished around 1280. The ruins of Ever Tower are tucked in close beside the bus station and a narrow alley runs south-west to Bath Lane.

Stowell Street is now Newcastle's China Town, lively and exotic but surrounded by some of the still run-down parts of the city. The ruins of the city walls are so tall that they throw a shadow over everything. There was a remote, distinct feeling of threat about the place. Morden Tower looked gloomy, but further along, where the wall turned south-west, Heber Tower had more space and looked pretty enough to be a picture postcard. Even so, the most authentic medieval feature of the West Walls was their oppressiveness.

Blackfriars, down Monk Street, had been renovated and integrated into a residential area. The cloister buildings of the Dominican friary have been put to contemporary use - gift shop, information centre and cafe. This was a welcome spot to get a cup of tea but delivered a sanitised dose of history. No wonder so many people fail to find the past exciting. Without an edge, a threat or a challenge, there is no substance to history.

Heber Tower

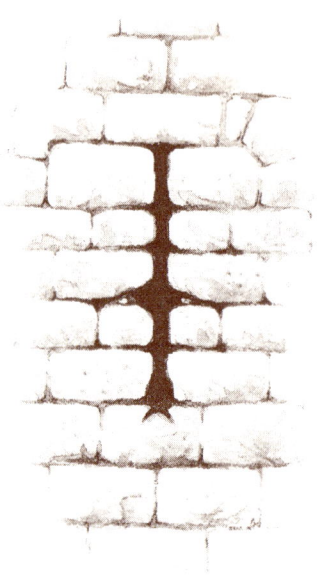

Arrow slit

Medieval Newcastle must have been a mixture of enterprise and fear. The walls must have brought security when they were built, so that not only were merchants attracted, but also abbots and friars, who built estates and gardens. For centuries the pattern of settlement was dictated by defence and the lie of the land. And it stayed that way for centuries.

Collingwood Bruce, whose nineteenth century book is still the standard field guide to Hadrian's Wall, wrote of his boyhood days: *"the town was almost entirely contained within the walls. The only exceptions were Sandgate, by the river's side, Northumberland Street, which, however, had many open spaces in it ...the west side of Percy Street (the east had scarcely a house upon it), a few houses in Gallowgate, and a clump of houses outside the west gate. All round about were gardens and green fields. Even inside the walls there were extensive tracts of open space and garden ground."*

It was within Bruce's lifetime that the town burst its skin and industry arrived. *"Beside all this"*, wrote Bruce, *"the air was fresh and wholesome."* The Newcastle Corporation of that day, though unreformed, objected to smoke.

Turning left at the end of Stowell Street, through a gap in the Town Walls and onto Bath Lane, it was possible to walk on the grass verge on the outer face of the walls, south-east past Durham Tower, to join Westgate Road. On the right of the junction was the old Waterloo pub, site of nineteenth century gallows. On the left was where the West Gate once stood. There are no earthly remains to mull over. Westgate Road, and the West Road beyond it, marks the course of Hadrian's Wall, but this part of the city, looking depressed and grubby, inspired little more than a backward glance on the way through.

Anyone making for the heart of present-day Newcastle would turn up Clayton Street and head toward Grey's Monument. It seemed perverse to be walking down Westgate Road.

On the right, on the site of a recently discovered Roman Wall turret, stood a modern Arts Centre. On the opposite side of the road, on the corner of Grainger Street, was St John's Church. In medieval times this was the church of the town traders, leaving St Andrew's to cater for the rural community.

West Wall: medieval masonary close to Durham Tower

Birch leaf

Until recently St John's was black with soot and in the winter the bare trees were a night roost for thousands of starlings. From a distance, and especially when picked out by Christmas lighting, the trees looked as if they were laden with exotic fruit. At close range the smell of the guano was overpowering. Now, soot, trees and starlings have all gone.

By Central Station, buried somewhere beneath the Miners' Institute, is another fragment of the Wall, and somewhere between Orchard Street and Clavering Place is a Roman cemetery. This sort of exploration, with nothing visible, is history for the professional or for those with a vivid imagination. It had begun to rain and people were scuttling for shop doorways. Along Collingwood Street, St Nicholas' Cathedral beckoned, but only for a fleeting visit. Inside, Collingwood Bruce's tomb maintained the link with the Wall, and there was a framed fragment of oak reputed to be from the Roman Bridge. Outside in the churchyard, down the path from Amen Corner, there was a plaque marking where Thomas Bewick's workshop once stood. The great wood engraver would have been an old man when Bruce was in his teens.

The High Level Bridge is the oldest surviving bridge on the Tyne as it flows through Newcastle. It was built in the 1840s and was opened by Queen Victoria. Viaducts, carrying the railway line from the bridge to the station and from the station to points north and east, slice across St Nicholas Street below the cathedral. Nineteenth century vision and confidence were apparent; the melee of road and rail, concrete and steel, obscured the fact that the ground fell away on three sides, leaving a natural promontory, and on this promontory stood the Norman Castle. This was the pivot of the town for 300 years, before the Town Walls were built.

Rowan leaf

The Keep was impregnable, at least until 10 am when a uniformed attendant opened the door. From inside it became obvious that much of the stonework had been restored, some well and some (such as in the chapel) with intrusive detail. Even so, there was a power and authority about the castle. It is easy to appreciate what it had been built for. In the words of Bruce, the Normans *"had dispossessed the nobles but they had not conquered the people. They were a handful of men amidst a host of enemies. Except when fully armed they were never safe."* The stone castle was built in the twelfth century to replace a wooden one (the original 'New Castle'), and by the end of the sixteenth century it was a ruin.

The Keep and its thirteenth century gatehouse are separated by the railway viaduct. Beneath its arches, cobbles marked out the position of missing walls and alleys. It took a few moments to realize that under the surface lay the mortal remains of the Roman headquarters at Pons Aelius. This was the fort that had protected the river crossing and was the original start of the Wall. It was an important place; the name Aelius was Hadrian's family name and would not have been bestowed lightly. Although there was even less to see on the ground than at Wallsend the impact was immediate. The railway had been built over the Norman ruins and medieval settlement. The Normans had built their forts on the site of a Saxon cemetery, which in turn had been built over the Roman fort of Pons Aelius. And doubtless there had been a British camp there before the Romans arrived. This clutter of cultures is what underpinned Newcastle's success as a city.

On the far side of the Keep was the Castle Garth or yard. After the demise of the castle this became a colourful corner of town; because of the absence of tolls and trade restrictions it was the resort of 'pedlars, grovers and chapmen', and was described in the early nineteenth century as a 'rag-fair'. On this morning, and particularly in the rain, it just looked empty. The Castle Stairs, between the Moot Hall and the South Curtain Wall, were steep and slippery, leading out onto Sandhill and the Quayside, opposite Neptune House. A few yards to the east lay the Swing Bridge.

The river swirled and slapped at the footings. It was hard to believe that there were salmon down there, pushing upstream through the turbid water. The Swing Bridge, red and white and reminiscent of the drain sluices of East Anglia or Zealand, was built in 1876 at the traditional bridging point of the river. This was where Pons Aelius had been. Gazing down from the boardwalk,

The Swing Bridge, site of the Roman bridge of Pons Aelius, on a wet start to the day.

half way to Gateshead, it was tempting to throw in a coin to join all the good-luck denaria in the muddy belly of the Tyne.

Back on the Newcastle shore, it was almost time to start the real business of the day, the walk west and out of the city. Having kept with the line of the Wall the previous day was reason enough to do the same on this day. However, knowing the West Road, and with the sky set for more rain, the prospect of the West End of Newcastle was not appealing. The alternative was to stay with the river, for at least a mile or two.

Sandhill, the scrap of land around the north end of the Swing Bridge, was the last historical knot worth unravelling in the city centre. It was another hotch-potch starting with the Romans. Their bridge probably lasted for centuries and there would have been a collection of houses there. In the thirteenth century a wooden bridge was burnt down and replaced by a stone one. This must have looked impressive; in the words of Daphne Rendel, writing in 1898, the twelve-arch structure *"was crowded with houses, and in the middle stood a tower with an iron gate, used by the Newcastle Corporation as a prison.... Near the northern or Newcastle end...was a great mound of sand, known as the Sandhill and used as a recreation ground by the burgesses when in sportive mood... Here stood the Guildhall and Maison Dieu."*

Eventually the bridge was washed away in a flood. By then the merchants, who lived in the beautiful row of three and four storey houses facing the quayside and Guildhall, had moved further up town. The Maison Dieu, or

St Catherine's Hospital, was founded in 1412 'for the support of nine poor men and four poor women.' It stood on the site of the present Guildhall.

The familiar Tyne Bridge, built in 1928, towers over the Sandhill and casts a distracting shadow.

Heading west at last, past the merchants' houses, the Waterside Hotel, under the High Level Bridge, past the half-timbered Cooperage and the modern Quayside Inn, the river threw off its shackles and swept ahead. This was merely an illusion, as the current flows in the other direction, but it was hard to tell the difference. The embankment has recently been paved for as far as the eye can see, and young plane trees planted. No-one was in sight. Walking past the Copthorne Hotel, through now heavy rain and with the swollen river just a few feet away to the left, it was disconcerting to look through the glass wall and see someone swimming in a heated pool, immune to the real elements outside.

The remaining city bridges followed in quick succession, first the elegant Queen Elizabeth II (Metro) Bridge, then the King Edward VII (rail) Bridge and finally the Redheugh (road) Bridge. After this the river swung to the right and the new embankment ran close beside Skinnerburn Road. The long rows of shrubs and trees still looked too new, neat and tidy, but at least they included alder, ash and aspen, natives whose ancestors might have clothed the valley slopes in Roman times.

On the other side of the road, stacked up into a palace of painted planks, was a set of pigeon lofts. How they had escaped a demolition order was a mystery. A middle-aged man wearing a plastic mac and Newcastle United cap called in his racers, making reassuring noises and jingling palmfuls of food. The birds came out of the sky like stooping peregrines, spiralling to land on the roof, then hopping straight inside. After a few minutes the man reappeared, having logged in the arrivals. There were another two to come, he explained. The race had been from London; 260 miles in 23 hours, but he wasn't expecting a win. His best bird was still missing and as he spoke his eyes raked the sky. Pigeon racing is a risky business, particularly for the pigeons.

There were no birds in sight over the river, not even a cormorant. The embankment was pristine, paved and bollarded. But nature was waiting in the wings. On the other side of the fence, on the steep ribbed facing of the artificial bank, were clumps of mayweed, fumitory and ragwort. Weeds are not so easy to exclude from the good life. Nor are rats. There were at least two on the

The Black Gate: 13th century gatehouse of Newcastle's Norman Castle.

A hanging doorway, behind the gatehouse.

The Cooperage, in the shadow of the High Level Bridge. The timbers are even more bent and twisted than they look.

water-line, though they quickly crept out of sight among the jetsam.

There were no rats in Britain in Roman times. In fact there were no rats in Italy or across the Empire. Black rats arrived from South-East Asia in the twelfth century, having taken advantage of easy transport. As new shipping lanes opened, so the rats appeared in sea-ports all over Europe. They brought the Black Death to Sunderland docks in 1349, and from there it spread across the region. They introduced the Great Plague of 1665, and destroyed a tithe of all the grain shipped from port to port. The brown rat, a bigger animal with broader head and smaller ears, arrived in the same way, and from the same part of the world, in the early eighteenth century. Over the past few decades the black rat has vanished from most of Britain, but the brown rat, which carries the same diseases, has adapted well to the enterprise culture.

Ragwort - one of the commonest quayside flowers.

Past the Business Park the paved embankment ended and there was a short stretch of simple riverside path. This veered right in front of a pylon and an outfall pipe, where brown liquid was being expelled into the still-abused Tyne. On the shelf of waste ground there was a vibrant yellow shroud of oilseed rape, as dense a crop as if it had been deliberately planted.

The path emerged onto William Armstrong Drive, close to the Armstrong Hotel, from where Scotswood Road leads west. The walk was not pleasant; the road was awash and there was no shelter. Every passing car sent a deluge splashing across the pavement, and in the row of breakers yards, patches of nettles and thistles were spangled with beads of rain.

It was a far cry from what Collingwood Bruce had found: *"To the west of town the Maiden's Walk, which is now represented by Scotswood Road, was to my mind unequalled for beauty by any spot on the earth's surface that I have seen.... I do not wonder that the few houses that were then built at the end of the Maiden's Walk were named Paradise."*

'Paradise' lay on the far side of the road, behind the Scotswood Deleval Drift Mine. The map had the name printed over an abattoir and engineering works, but these had been superseded by the Whitehouse Enterprise Centre.

The Vickers Armstrong Works takes up the rest of the riverside as far as Scotswood Bridge. The great grey shed gave no clue as to what was on the production line inside, but at the far corner the doors were open and a Challenger Tank was pirouetting like a circus elephant in front of some boiler-suited technicians. A smell of scorched paint drifted through the wire fences.

At the junction by Scotswood Bridge there was a subway, which was dingy but came out on the north side of Scotswood Road by a bank of wild flowers. The colours were bright and clean; discs of cadmium and chrome yellow, Oxford ragwort and dandelion shone out among others of magenta and carmine, red and white campion.

Climbing the bank led up onto the old railway line, where there were patches of plantain and horsetail. From here, after a short walk along the trackway, it would be possible to turn up Denton Road. Wishing to keep in touch with the line of Hadrian's Wall, which runs along the top of the valley and through Benwell, a detour up to the West Road at Denton Bank would lead to the first visible remains of the Wall. Rather than head up Denton Road however, there was a green alternative via Denton Dene.

A path led out across open grassland behind the Sporting Arms, then down into the cleft of the dene. A thick canopy of trees filled the hollow ahead. The presence of steep-sided, heavily wooded valleys or denes must have been a consideration when the Wall was being planned. Enemies would have found it easy to hide in them and attack at a weak point, hence the Wall had to be set above them on the ridge.

A metalled track ran up the cleft and into the woodland. Everything to do with the city was immediately shut out. There were steep banks on either side, rock outcrops and gnarled tree roots. Oak boughs reached out to touch each other overhead. It looked like a scene from a Bewick print. It was also the perfect place for an ambush, whether by Picts on Romans or today's attackers on today's victims.

Sycomore seedling

Oak Leaf

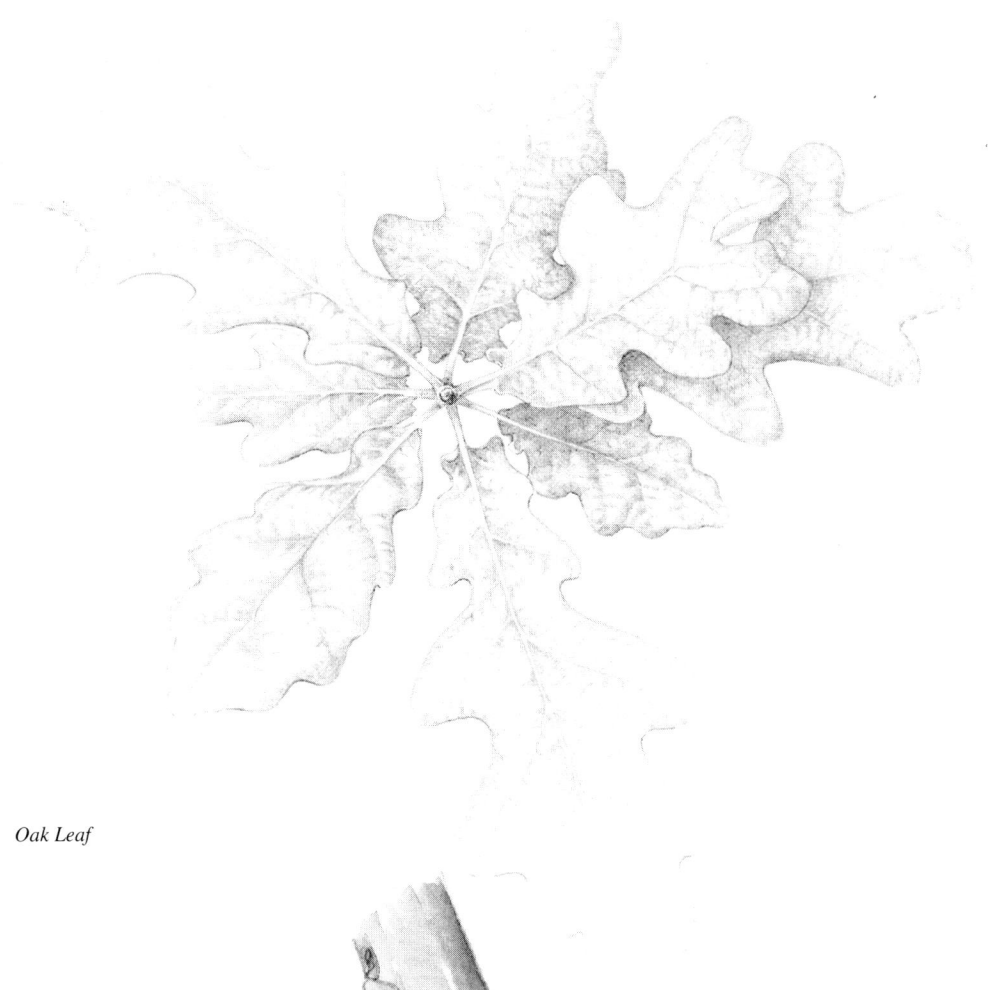

Faced Wall

For all its wildwood atmosphere the dene ended abruptly, its head and shoulders obliterated by Broadwood Road and Newcastle suburbs. But after a steady climb the ground levelled and there were side-streets with Roman names to show that the Wall was close. Turret Road still led to a turret.

Anyone familiar with the A69 knows the stretch of Wall on the grass verge out of Denton, but coming upon it from the south side, head on, with the main road on the other side, gave it an unexpected atmosphere. The complete stretch measured 78 paces long. Only two or three of the lower courses remained, reaching no more than knee height. The turret was bare and bleak, and the rubble core had been bound by Department of the Environment (DoE) rather than Roman mortar, but the ruined wall still had character and resonance. It was still the Wall. Approaching on foot, alone and in the rain, paid a modest dividend. The passing traffic was all on the Barbarian side.

On the opposite side of the road, hidden by a new bank and wall, lay Denton Hall. It was built in the early seventeenth century and still has a Cromwellian air of cold simplicity. In its heyday it was the home of Lady Mary Wortley Montague, friend of Dr Johnson and Sir Joshua Reynolds. It also was, and perhaps still is, the home of a ghost known as Silky. Not content with appearing to foretell death, the ghost, in the shape of a woman, has been known to stand in doorways and touch people in the middle of the night, 'leaving a touch felt with pain for days'. One night in 1884 Silky was reported as being heard 'dragging something through two unoccupied rooms, down a flight of stairs, to a window which was flung open'. The mystery was never solved. The hall is now called Bishop's House and is the residence of the Catholic Bishop of Hexham and Newcastle.

The Hall, and the Wall, now lie only a few yards away from a different kind of monster, the Western Bypass. A footbridge offered a safe way over the traffic, but before heading west a quick walk in the opposite direction, down the West road and past the Co-op, allowed a look at the most easterly fragment of the Wall. This lay in the forecourt of a filling station on the corner of Denton Road.

People bustled about getting petrol, in too much of a hurry to cast a glance at the stonework poking out of the pavings. It was only a few inches high and there was no notice to warn of its significance. There was a slightly bigger fragment a few steps back down the road, in a wired enclosure in front of Charlie Brown's Autocentre. It seemed very British, taking understatement to this extreme.

The first Wall fragment on the roadside out of Newcastle, in the forecourt of a filling station.

The footbridge over the Western Bypass had a fragile grace all of its own. It was made of concrete but felt like a rope-walk over a precipice of streaming traffic. The West Road, the A69 to Hexham and Carlisle, gathers pace beyond the roundabout; most cars accelerate up the hill and are travelling at speed when they pass the last Wall fragment out of the city.

It is nine feet thick, part of the earliest phase of building. After this there was no reason to stay with the main road, and next to the footbridge on Avalon Road a gate and path led down into Sugley Dene.

The steepness of the slope into the dene came as a surprise. Tall beech trees, straight as cathedral columns, reached up out of its depth, spreading their boughs into Gothic arches and masking the sky. At the bottom was a burn and pathway, running south towards the Tyne. Oak trees joined the beeches as the steepness of the slopes eased. Jays and a greater spotted woodpecker called from the canopy.

Woodland turned to parkland, with a seam of hawthorn and willow to mark the path of the burn until south of Neptune Drive. After that the dene narrowed again and houses closed in on either side, so that the way was blocked and the only option was to follow a parallel road. This was Dene Avenue, a badly designed Council estate with many stray dogs. The nearby Sugley Dene must have been the secret adventure world for most children on the estate.

At the bottom of the dene were redbrick terraces and an old vicarage and railway station. These had been restored and renovated into private homes and gardens, very different from Dene Avenue. The branch railway line had been renovated too, forming one of the few completed stretches of a cycle/walkway carrying the new Hadrian's Wall National Trail.

The railway line provided an easy route westwards, made memorable by the rain at last easing and finally stopping, after more than five hours. Blackbirds came out of the brambles and sang with joy.

Feathers from the back of a female pheasant.

Lemington looked much better under a sky streaked with silver. The railway line followed the foot of the Tyne valley, below the massive reclamation project of the Percy Pit. The landscape was lunar and the trackway, not yet surfaced, was coated in a slurry of fly ash. Soon there will be grass underfoot and thousands of shrubs on the slopes. Already a few self-set hawthorns had got things started.

Beech leaves:
mines made by tiny weevil

Smooth-barked beech tree, Sugley Dene.

It would have been a good place to stop awhile, have a late lunch and a look back at the day. Tyneside had been both worse and better than expected, caught in the continuous act of changing fast. But the prospect of resting or reflecting was made unappealing by sodden clothes.

Hawthorn - May blossom in its prime, before the petals start to fall.

The old railway crosses Lemington Road, past a huge half-derelict building clad in corrugated iron and rotten planks. It was being used as a breakers' yard according to the sign, but only pigeons could be heard clattering about in the vast space inside.

On the far side of the Tyne was the Stella Power Station. The haughs or levels on both sides of the river were drained for industrial use but are still not completely dry. Along the track were marshy hollows full of canary grass, and sallow bushes which would be bright with catkins in the spring. An old spider web in a broken pipe still held the body of a Hebrew character moth, the sallow's chief pollinator.

Newburn was also in the throws of reclamation, and new business plots were being cleared in the shadow of Stella North. Across the single-lane bridge from the village stood Ryton.

Had the weather been kinder it would have been good to walk across to the little nature reserve at Ryton Willows, where the pools are rich in aquatic life. The miniature water lily called frog-bit probably still occurred there and might be in flower. But it was a chilly afternoon and it looked a long way. Soon it would be time to leave the valley and make for the Wall as it enters Northumberland. Past the Tyne Rowing Club and the Leisure Centre a bridleway led off the road and through Newburn Country Park.

It was at this point that the countryside arrived. Looking up to Hallow Hill a farm was visible, with sheep and horses in the fields. The fields were corrugated in 'rigg and furrow' patterns, the marks of the three-field system, ploughed the same way for centuries. There were buttercups from corner to corner.

Along the bridleway, beside the Reigh Burn, there were beds of reedmace, yellow flag and bur-reed. Wasps were visiting figwort flowers, and a green-veined white butterfly was sitting with wings half open on a comfrey leaf. The burn was swollen with milky water; sewage was discharging into it from somewhere upstream.

Eventually the bridleway met a track, leading uphill and past a plantation with some big ash and wych elm trees. A few of the elms were dead but most looked in good health; no tell-tale signs of Dutch Elm Disease, such as the withering of leaves at the ends of the upper branches. The track headed up to Coach Road, past hedgerow oaks and banks of tufted vetch and jack-by-the-hedge. At the top was Wellfield Wood, with a useful viewpoint notice made by local schoolchildren. The view across the Tyne valley, and back into Newcastle, was excellent in the rain-cleared air.

Hexham Road, between Throckley and Heddon, runs straight as a die. This, and the commanding view of the Tyne valley, were the obvious clues that the road followed the line of the Wall. The valley route out of Newcastle had

Wych elm leaf. The shape and serrations vary from one tree to the next.

certainly been more interesting than the West Road, but it still felt much better to be standing full square on the Roman defences again.

There was no stonework to be seen, and at first no earthworks either. The terrain of the first field on the left was obscured by a crop of oilseed rape, and the second was almost as hidden under winter barley. But there was a shadow in the cobalt green of the barley, and beyond the drive to Heddon Hall this resolved itself into the unmistakable groove or ditch which is the remains of the Vallum.

The first view of the Vallum ditch, in pastureland to the west of Throckley.

The Vallum was a system of bank-ditch-bank running parallel with the Wall but some distance to the south. Exactly what it was for is a mystery, but it probably marked a military exclusion zone. The word 'vallum' comes from Bede and means wall, which is confusing since it is used exclusively to describe the ditch system.

Antiquaries, the amateur archaeologists of the eighteenth and nineteenth centuries, thought the Vallum had been built by Hadrian and the Wall by Severus, and that Hadrian's ditch augmented one created by Agricola. Travellers like William Hutton (who walked the Wall in 1801 at the age of 78) must have wasted a good deal of time trying to sort it out. Coming out of Newcastle Hutton wrote in his diary, in obvious excitement; *"Fifty yards on my left, down a green pasture, run, in bold figures, the united works of Agricola and Hadrian, dressed in about half their antient grandeur; and, having*

*Barley-heads; the seed-cases have not filled out and the long awns are still pointing upwards.
A few weeks to go to ripening.*

this clue, we can trace them over the inclosures for many miles." And so we still can. It felt good to walk on open pasture and to explore the Vallum as the redoubtable Hutton had done.

On the rising ground into Heddon-on-the-Wall, in a green field to the left of the road, was the first really good piece of Wall to have escaped the road-makers and farm-builders of the eighteenth century. Most of the facing stone had gone, but the core rose several feet in height, bound in the firm DoE mortar again rather than the puddled clay the Romans would have used. It was a very impressive sweep of Wall, 256 paces in length with a medieval kiln hollowed out at the western end.

An impressive stretch of the Wall, looking east towards Heddon.

The thrill of setting hand and foot on the stonework was marred by the sensation of being watched. A bus was parked in the layby alongside and it was impossible to shrug off the feeling that idle eyes were following every move. It was galling to discover a few minutes later that the bus was empty, but that the driver had been watching from the gate at the top of the village. He was surprisingly chatty. Did I know about the stone axes dug up from under the greenhouse down the road? Had I seen the dead badger on the road by Throckley Church? It would have been worth going on a bus ride just for the conversation.

Opposite the Three Tuns a road ran on with houses on one side and a V-shaped ditch on the other. The ditch was another part of the Roman defences, a deep trench immediately to the north of the Wall. The Wall itself was buried under the road.

After swinging off course for a few hundred yards to cross the A69, the Military Road began to climb in a straight line to find the highest ridge and the way west. The Vallum and Ditch were so cleanly cut that they could have been dug with a JCB. Rudchester Farm stood on the left. At this point the road ran straight through Vindovala, the fourth fort from Wallsend.

Hutton described it as *"a close, joining the road, of five acres, now in grass, and eminently situated, (with) the strong marks of former buildings, and still stronger of its ramparts."*

Had it been early in the day it would have been easier to get excited about the tussocks and shallow trenches that still remain of the fort. It has been excavated, but not extensively, and yielded a rich assortment of shrines and a Mithraic Temple. It was a pity not to be moved or enthused. The farm was built out of stone from the Wall and there were supposed to be fragments of inscriptions to be found, and a pit nearby called the Giant's Grave which was something to do with the civilian settlement. This should have been worth a few minutes of exploration, but the light had drained out of the day and there was a sudden chill in the air.

Back on the road it was hard to know exactly what had gone wrong. Harlow Hill was the finishing point of the second day and getting there had become the over-riding goal.

An hour later, having reached Harlow Hill and eaten a good meal, things looked different. It would have been possible to go back to Rudchester. Instead, and perhaps as a reaction to thinking so much about the past, Whittle Dene Reservoirs offered the chance of a quiet dusk-watch for birds.

Whittle Dene runs down to the Tyne at Ovingham and gathers the waters of a host of little streams, such as the Bogle Burn and Sparrow Letch. Astride the road to the west of Harlow Hill the headwaters have been impounded into a series of pools, of which the biggest is the Great North Reservoir.

Summer is not the best time of year to expect waterbirds, which was lucky because there was very little water in the upper pools. The Great North Reservoir had been drained for repair work, and the dry bed was covered with

*The Military Road,
following the line of the Wall towards Halton.*

Wing feathers from a curlew.

weeds. At first there seemed to be nothing moving. With the failing light, the colours were turning to earth tones. Suddenly two hares appeared - they may have been there all the time - and there were a few lapwings and an oystercatcher beside the runnel in the middle of the basin. The oystercatcher was noisy and skittish and it was a relief when it left. The hares worked their way across the bed of weeds, digging out roots of orache and red-leg and leaving swathes of foliage. A small group of curlews landed, bathed together in the shallow runnel, then split up into twos and threes to feed and roost. After a few minutes it was impossible to see them against the mud.

For a moment the sky was alive with swifts and martins, hawking for insects over the full pools. Then the swifts turned into noctule bats and the day was finished. Somewhere over the trees by Harlow Hill a woodcock called on a roding flight. Jupiter appeared in the west sky, followed by Saturn and Mars and the brighter stars.

Tail feathers from a woodcock.

*Dead meadow pipit, picked up from the Military Road.
The plumage is a delicate mixture of earth colours.*

3 Harlow Hill - Chollerford

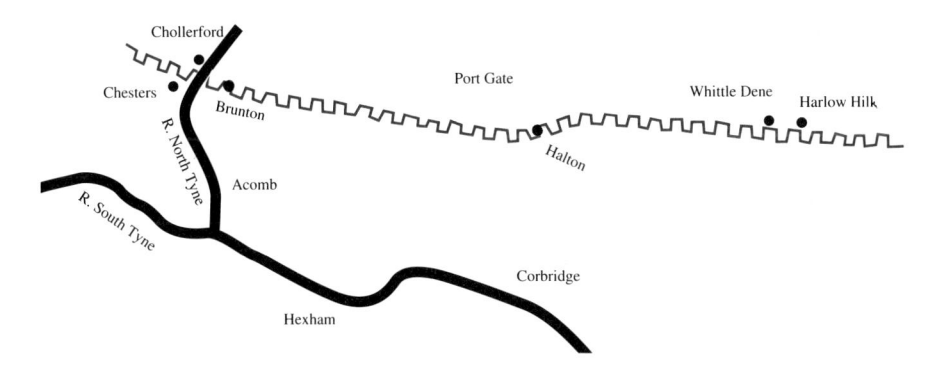

Harlow Hill - Chollerford: 12 miles

Long straight roads are usually credited to the Romans. The Stanegate, Agricola's east-west highway forged in the early years of the Roman occupation, runs to the south through Corbridge to cross Dere Street, the up-country route from York, at the supply base of Corstopitum. When the Wall was built it was supplied from the Stanegate using the network of earlier forts; there was no need for a major new road.

Westward from Whittle Dene, the B6318 runs so straight and true that it is difficult not to read it as part of the same master-plan. But that would be to deny the Wall, for it is the Wall that should trace this determined line.

The metalled ribbon of road was edged by trenches and rows of trees, hiding the Vallum and Ditch, and by farmhouses or steadings one after another as far as the eye could see. These were all made of stone plundered from the Wall, carted away by farmers who had more to think about than the whims of posterity. After the scare of the Jacobite rebellion in 1745 the government also had a hand in the obliteration of a bit of our national heritage. When Bonnie Prince Charlie marched south to threaten Carlisle General Wade couldn't get his artillery across from Newcastle because of the lack of a good road, the Stanegate having disappeared long ago. Thus, when the uprising had been put down Wade had a new road built, and the obvious line to follow was that of the Wall. For much of its length, and certainly where the engineering was easy, the new Military Road used the existing foundations. It was a model of resource management and conservation.

From the crest of the hill, with the reservoirs of Whittle Dene shining like shards from a broken mirror, the road ran fast and true. The speed of the cars was too fast to make it a comfortable walk. Early morning traffic sped by, setting swathes of cow parsley dancing in its wake. The Military Road is probably more dangerous now than in Wade's day, or in the last century when footpads and highwaymen lent it a dangerous reputation.

All around, fields of barley and rape shone with the brightness of chemical dyes. Beyond East Wallhouses and the Robin Hood Inn the Wall ditch, to the right of the road, was deep and sharp-sided, first grass-lined and then wooded. Plantations to the north, bearing names like Sparrowletch and Foulhoggers, also served to break up the profile.

At South Clarewood, in a pasture just south of the farm, a man was working a collie, but the dog was young and the sheep wary. Further on at Carr Hill a tenant farmer of the Blackett estate was tagging a cow, holding it firm between the lee side of a shed and a galvanized gate while he stapled a yellow plastic label through its ear. Several other cows stood close by, all Hereford x Friesians. Normally this is a good-natured and dull cross-breed capable of nothing more menacing than chewing off its neighbour's ear tag, but there were new-born calves in the field and the man had a collie which was sitting on the far side of the fence and attracting their attention. As the cows drew closer the collie looked uneasily to her master. He was talking, looking south-west into the valley and pointing out the farms in the estate, from Aydon to Matfen. It had been a good year for lambing, he said; the cold winter had helped. He enjoyed working on these wide pastures at the crest of the valley: *"every day a breeze in your hair"*. Finally, he noticed the plight of the collie and called her to him. By then she was surrounded by the hostile beasts and glad to move, but she had not complained and would have sat tight until they had trampled her.

The Wall defences rippled across the field west of Carr Hill, so that cattle and calves were hidden from view in the ditch or behind the mounds of the Vallum. At Down Hill the route of the Wall crossed a knoll, the Vallum swung to the south and the Military Road detoured to the north. Hence the knoll stood aloof and had become an enclosed spinney, hiding the Wall foundations and quarries in briars and brambles. The view from the Vallum mounds was excellent, the air washed clean by passing showers borne on blustery winds. To the south lay the lands surrounding medieval Aydon Castle, then the Tyne and the course of Dere Street as it approaches the river-crossing at Corstopitum. On the far skyline lay Dipton Wood, the Shire and the edge of the Durham Moors.

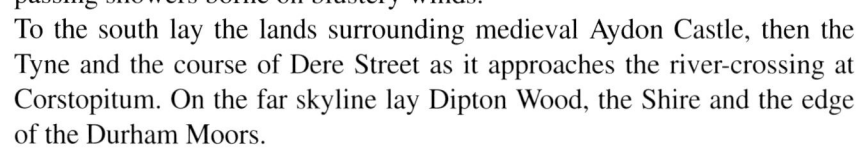

The close-cropped turf of the Vallum had been scorched by the wind but there were sheltered hollows and one particularly comfortable sun-spot where a fox had been sitting until quite recently, leaving behind a distinctive scent and a flattened bed of yarrow. He was probably in the spinney now.

Flowers fare badly on farmland, edged out by more efficient crop production. Nitrogen fertilizers have encouraged quick-growing grasses at the expense of traditional herbs. In 1956 a writer called David Harrison passed this way and noticed the flowers: *"The hedgerows and meadows were as attractive as any garden border and all the more so for being undesigned. Buttercups and cow parsley, of course, were everywhere, also deep red clover, plenty of cranesbill and the trefoil which carpets every odd corner with its yellow bird's feet......: but there were kingcups as well, shy pansies, ragged robin, wild mignonette, sorrel, translucent red in the bright sun, and, in larger clumps, dog roses and yellow broom brilliant after the rain. I almost wished I were a botanist,.....though I have always thought that flowers are best left to the poets."*

Cranesbill

All the flowers mentioned by Harrison were still to be seen along the road verge, the ancient berm or space between the Wall and the ditch, but the fields around must have been a prettier sight in the post-war years, even allowing for poetic licence. The push to increase the stock-holding capacity of this marginal land has led to a monotony of detail. Still, things are changing fast; phrases like 'set-aside' and 'stewardship' have entered the language and may spell a reprieve for haymeadows and buttercup-studded pastures.

The three common buttercups; left to right, bulbous buttercup creeping buttercup, and meadow buttercup.

The mounds and ditch of the Vallum act like rigg and furrow, creating places for different flowers. Of these, buttercups were the most prominent, as is always the case in Northumberland once the dandelions have seeded. At the top of the slope at Down Hill there were drifts of bulbous buttercups, short-stemmed and with sepals folded back. Further down the slope, on damper soil, were the taller meadow buttercups, and at the bottom were creeping buttercups.

Back on the road and heading west again, it would have been easy to miss the next fort, Haltonchesters, for there was little about it to catch or hold the imagination. It was called Onnum by the Romans; the name means The Rock, perhaps inspired by the most obvious landscape feature of Down Hill. It was a cavalry fort, and was built some time after the Wall, so a gap had to be created for it.

Down Hill, looking west. mounds and ditch of Vallum in foreground

In the middle of the fort, on the left of the road, were the gates of Halton Castle, from where an avenue of sycamores marched south to the ruins of a thirteenth century tower-house. This too was built from Roman stone, which accounts once again for the levelled, lumpy condition of the fort. On the north side of the road was a very flat plateau of pasture which was once called 'Brunt ha'penny field' and which must at some time in its early ploughing have yielded some blackened coins. Onnum (or Hunnum, or Onno, depending on the reference used) was a disappointment.

There was something vital about Stagshaw; perhaps it was the way the road swept down to the modern roundabout, or the fact that it was here that Dere Street, the road to the wilderness, crossed the Wall. How many legionaries would have marched north expecting to be home by the year end? Portgate, the fortified gateway, marked the beginning of what was bandit country. It stood between what is now the roundabout and the Errington Arm Inn.

The Military Road west of Portgate still follows the line of the Wall, through much poorer country, wetter and drier by turns and 100 metres higher than the arable farmland to the east. The Vallum disappeared into a dense plantation, spruce at one end and pine at the other, with a sprinkling

West towards Stagshaw. The pale fields are crops of oil seed rape.

of beech and birch in between. There were some chewed cones indicating that squirrels were about, some signs of roe deer, and what looked like a sparrow-hawk kill, a circlet of pigeon feathers around a cut stump. Sparrow-hawks pluck their prey carefully before feeding. There was dew

Spruce cone, stripped by a red squirrel to get at the seeds.

on the feathers, so the pigeon must have been breakfast, almost certainly for a female hawk. After the constant noise of the wind the silence of Stanley Plantation was profound. If there were deer about they were keeping down among the brashings.

Back out in the sharp sunlight, on the south side of the plantation, Fawcett Hill and Hangman's Hill lay in the foreground, shielding the Tyne valley. The Vallum crossed the top of the Hexham road, through an area of heathland, its ditch covered in gorse.

Gorse is usually taken as a sign of ancient cultivation, where farmers won and lost the fight to grow meagre crops of rye. Here, the Vallum was the initial cause of the breaking of the ground and the gorse may already have been in place by the Dark Ages. Alternatively, the whole area around Stagshaw Bank may have suffered from overgrazing in the centuries when it served as a cattle fair and gathering ground for cross-border drovers.

Linnets ('linties') were calling from the prickly depth of the gorse bushes. Bumblebees fumbled about among the clumps of chrome-yellow flowers, but the cold breeze had made them slow and irritable. There was no lazy drone, and no heavy coconut scent to cast a spell and slow the pace of the summer.

Fawcett Hill, north of Corbridge. The line of the Wall is just beyond the skyline.

At Hill Head Farm the road leaves the Wall, switching to the left and then the right of it before dropping down into the valley of the North Tyne. Hill Head looked busy, although no-one was about. These days, farms are run by skeleton crews of tractor-drivers rather than communities of farm-hands; the buildings often lie deserted for weeks on end. High up beside the east window of the farm-house it was possible, through binoculars, to make out an inscribed stone, CHO V11 > CAECILI CLIIME, proof if any were needed that the place was built from plundered stone. Caecilius Clemens was the centurion of the eighth cohort; every stretch of Wall bore a centurial stone to identify its team of builders, proud of their achievement or relieved to have finished their task.

The detour by the Military Road off the foundations didn't serve to preserve the Wall, which suffered so badly at the hands of the road-builders in the 1750s that nothing is visible in the big field to the west of the farm. Local land-owners, who saw the Wall as a long-term resource for building stone, were as horrified by the actions of General Wade's

Roman inscription in the stonework of Hill Head.

men as were antiquaries such as Reverend Stukeley, who described them as 'senseless animals' engaged in 'vile havoc'. However, this sweep of pasture, called Hefenfelt, has more of a story to tell than just the Wall.

In the Dark Ages Britain was separated into warring kingdoms, of which Northumbria and Mercia were among the most powerful. At Doncaster in the year 633 Edwin, English king of Northumbria, was defeated by the alliance of Penda of Mercia and the Celtic king Cadwallon of Gwynedd. Northumbria soon split apart into the older kingdoms of Bernicia and Deira, ruled by Edwin's nephews Osric and Eanfrith. When they were duly defeated or murdered by Cadwallon, things looked black for the north and for Christianity. Fortunately there was a hero at hand; Oswald, younger brother of Eanfrith, who had spent most of his life with the monks of Iona. In 635 he landed at the old Northumbrian capital of Bamburgh and marched south to gather an army. Meanwhile, the battle-hardened Cadwallon and his Celts marched north up Dere Street and set up camp in Hexham.

Oswald was outnumbered, untested, but clever. He was also a devout Christian. The evening before the inevitable battle he set up a cross on the site of what is now St Oswald's chapel, on the brow of Hefenfelt (Heavenfield). It would then have been a bare ridge. In the morning Cadwallon led a daunting force up the hill out of Tynedale, but he could not attack directly because of the Wall. This stood at its original height of over 16 feet, an impossible barrier. He was forced to attack from the north-west, up the steepest slope of the hill. His advantage in numbers counted for nothing and he lost the battle. The fighting ranged far and wide; the fanatical Christians followed the fleeing Celts and cut them down. One of the bloodiest clashes took place just south of the Wall and the road in what is now the field called Mould's Close. Cadwallon was killed a few miles to the south, heading for Wales.

Penda killed Oswald a few years later and it took centuries, plus the Normans, to unite the nation. But in gratitude for his success against Cadwallon, Oswald invited the monks of Iona to establish a monastery at Lindisfarne.

At the roadside is a small lay-by and a cross, and a County Council information panel. There are no signs or notices at the little chapel which is hidden in a cluster of tall trees, or in the field or over the Wall foundations.

Looking west across the North Tyne Valley, from Planetrees. Chesters is to the right on the west bank of the river.

The Military Road sidesteps Planetrees Farm, crossing to the north side of the Wall on the steep slope of the hill. Full canopies of trees, including beech, oak and sycamore (the planetree of the place-name) hid the views to the north for the first time. The outlook would have been even more enclosed if most of the wych elms had not died. Dutch elm disease took a long time to reach the isolated, non-suckering northern elms, but the result has been just as dramatic. Several tall skeletons on the old field-edge swayed and creaked, taking the full force of the wind and threatening to topple at any moment. Looking at such a waste it is no comfort to know that the disease has been around for thousands of years. The 'Elm Decline' of bio-historical text-books used to be blamed on neolithic farmers. By Roman times it was a scarce tree, as it will be again.

On the right of the road lay the entrance to Brunton Quarry, a wonderful place for orchids and dingy skipper butterflies, but private and needing more time than was available. On the left was a stile leading to a stretch of Wall, the first since Heddon and therefore important. Unfortunately it was imprisoned in a post and wire fence and made sterile by preservation. This made it doubly difficult to imagine the state it must have been in when William Hutton passed in 1801. Having walked all the way from Birmingham to see the Wall he must have been incensed to find it being dismantled before his eyes.

Land-owner Henry Tulip was having a new farm-house built and his labourers were in the middle of taking up the stones. Hutton sent a message *"to give my compliments to Mr Tulip, and request him to desist"*. Hutton is therefore credited with having saved this stretch of the Wall, but

Sketches of a male hawfinch The parkland around Hexham is a favoured habitat.

no-one he met on his travels took him very seriously and it seems more likely that Mr Tulip simply ignored the eccentric old man and left what stone he didn't need.

As usual, the Vallum was a more dramatic feature than the Wall, not only in Planetrees Field but across the next pasture, which fell sharply to a grown-out hedge. Scrambling through this, and stepping down a bank of tree roots and big boulders which might have belonged in the Wall, a sea of barley lay ahead. After so much pastureland this was an arresting sight, made more beautiful as the ripening ears danced to every inflection of the wind.

Trees marked the course of the North Tyne at the foot of the valley, and on the far side a cobwebbing of hedges rather than walls separated the meadows and coverts. The course of the Wall, the only straight line running against the grain of the valley, was clear from Chesters up to Walwick. On the skyline to the left was Warden Hill, capped by an Iron

Age hill fort. The ramparts were clear even from this distance. What happened to it when the Romans arrived? Most hill forts only contained two or three huts and the defences seem out of proportion with the needs of an economy based on grazing a few cattle and goats.

Half way down the side of the valley the Military Road kinks to the north-west to cross the North Tyne at Chollerford Bridge rather than at the Roman abutments half a mile to the south. This and the presence of Brunton House is probably why several good fragments of Wall have survived, most notably around Brunton Turret. A lay-by off the A6079 allows tourist-friendly access up the hill to the turret and a good stretch of Wall, standing at head height.

Close behind the Wall lay a shelter-belt of tall trees which housed a lively colony of red squirrels. Most population studies of the decreasing red squirrel have shown that it does best in large conifer forests, but the population density here must have been well above the national average of two per acre. There are squirrels about more often than not, and there

Brunton turret.

was one now nuzzling in the afternoon shadows. It was very brightly coloured, a sign that it was young and had probably only left the drey in April. Adult red squirrels vary in redness through the year; they moult their body-fur twice, in spring and autumn, but the ear and tail fur is moulted only once, in early autumn. This means that the bushy ears and tail get more and more bleached and threadbare, even in early summer when the rest of the body is a fiery russet.

Downhill from Brunton Bank lay the abutments which once carried the Wall over the North Tyne. The only path to it was from Chollerford Bridge, along the line of the old North British Railway. The prospect of cheap coal, from the Plashetts mine now buried beneath Kielder Water, made the railway company an attractive investment in 1862, but the mines were too out-of-the-way to thrive, and a passenger service only delayed closure until the Beeching cuts of the 1960s. Natural forces had been at work since then and the stretch down-river to Hexham had become a paradise of flowers and bird song. In most places the only clue to the path's history was its level surface, but tucked into the bank below the bridge were the remains of a goods wagon, once used as a hay store.

Two stone piers of the Roman bridge sometimes appear out of the depth of the river, but not on this particular evening. On the far side was the bath-house of Chesters Fort and the excavations of the east abutment, still in progress. The west bank, with its complex and impressive stoneworks, was excavated in 1860 by John Clayton who lived at Chesters. His 'antiquarian enthusiasm' saved a great deal of the Wall; it spoilt a lot too but it seems mean to carp. He spent his whole life amassing inscriptions and artifacts, excavating forts and milecastles, and rebuilding bits of the Wall. Thus we now have not just Hadrian's Wall, but Clayton's Wall.

One of the great joys about the Wall is that nobody really knows very much about it and every expert so far has been proved wrong in one way or another. Old William Hutton assumed that Hadrian had built the Vallum and Severus the Wall; academic opinion was quite clear and

Hutton, like all true enthusiasts, believed what he was told. By Clayton's day there were new theories to account for what he found, but he still got the bridge wrong. He discovered, by his excavations of the abutments, that there had been two bridges, and he ascribed the first to Agricola and the second to Hadrian. It now seems that the first bridge bore the Wall and was therefore Hadrianic, whilst the second bridge came some time later and bore a road. Whatever the theories, the fallen bridge carries with it an ambience of mystery and it was good to sit amongst the shattered stones of the tower and mill-race, and try to find the phallus, an item of good-luck graffiti carved onto the upstream face of the abutment.

This made a point for finishing the Roman part of the day, but the long evening ahead left time to detour south and explore the river.

The North Tyne is a handsome river, fast and shallow in places where white-water rapids cut through or cover shelves of sandstone and whinstone, slow and indigo-deep where it runs by parkland and hangers

Footpath through hazel and oak woodland, between Chollerford and Acomb on the old railway line.

of oak and beech. Although the headwaters have been dammed at Kielder its sinuous course, from Falstone down to the Meeting of the Waters at Warden, is still ruled by natural forces rather than the Water Company. It flows as it chooses and there are banks of boulders and tree-roots which would not be tolerated along the tamed rivers of the south.

Otter spraint on a moss-covered sandstone slab above the river North Tyne.

The lower reach of the river has been the territory of what is almost certainly the same otter for the last ten years. This time there were no otter footprints along the sand-shelves on the heel of the river. Otters are water creatures and rarely patrol the banks for more than a few paces at a time, unlike mink. But there was better luck further along, where a line of beeches were under-cut and their knotted roots laid bare. Here, one of the key sprainting posts was in use. Otter droppings ('spraints') are a gluey mix of fish-bones and green jelly. They stick fast to rocks or tree-stumps and give off a strong scent, acting as a signpost for any potential mate or rival. The scent is of cod-liver-oil-and-musk, not unpleasant. This particular spraint, on a sandstone boulder, was old and half washed away, so it was grey and the fish bones showed through. They were eel bones, which was as well for there was an old-fashioned bailiff about, who might have resented the taking of trout or salmon.

Dippers

Discovering that the otter was still on the river was immensely satisfying. It was a magical evening, cold and still. As the light began to fade a duck goosander flew upstream, followed minutes later by two young dippers.

Back on the old railway line, with flowers of wood cranesbill adding splashes of mauve to the white of wood anemones and the lemon-yellow of late primroses, there was time to stop and see how everything changed

Primroses on the bank of the old railway line.

with the twilight. It was impossible to stand still for long without shivering. On an overhanging birch twig an early seed-cone resolved itself into one of the most beautiful of moths, a lesser swallow prominent. It was too early in the night for it to be on the wing, and perhaps it would not fly at all because of the cold.

*Lesser swallow prominent moth. Shades of brown on the wings.
The 'fur' of the thorax can be either grey or dark chocolate.*

4 Chollerford - Haughton Common

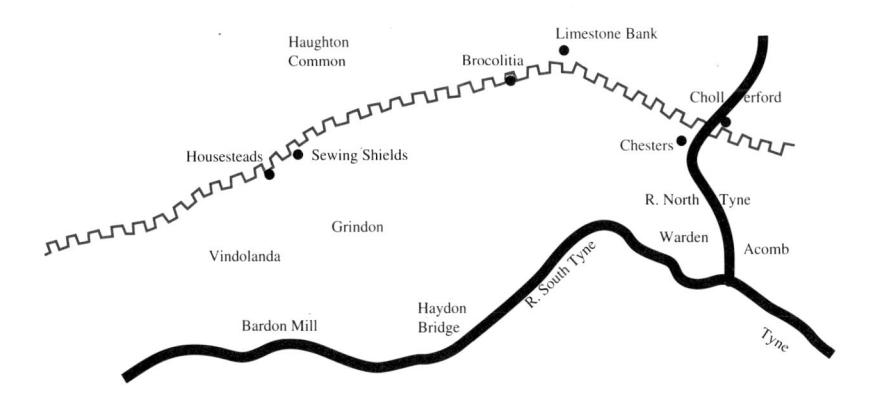

Chollerford - Hawkside/Haughton: 11 1/2 miles

A family of goosanders was on the river upstream of Chollerford bridge, exploring the eddies and backwaters. The mother was preening, settled on a boulder from where she could keep watch over seven ducklings.

Goosanders are now a common sight on the Tyne. In the late winter they gather in pairs on the broader reaches of the river before moving upstream to find nesting sites. The drakes are big and brightly coloured, quite out of place when camouflage is called for, but by the time the eggs are hatched they have left on a moult migration and it is the smaller ducks that rear the young. Life is cheap along the river and duckling appears on the menu of most predators. To have half-raised seven was an achievement.

The mother goosander was alert to any hint of danger. When a wood pigeon clattered overhead she drew in her feathers and slid into the water, swimming out into the open current with just her spiky head and neck visible. The ducklings had taken their cue and vanished.

The cause of the disturbance turned out to be an angler, a fly-fisherman in waders and Barbour jacket. The North Tyne is famous for its salmon and sea trout; people pay a lot of money for the privilege of a day on the river. Riparian owners look to their bailiffs to make the most of fish stocks, and given a free hand many bailiffs would treat goosanders as vermin.

Above the weir at Chollerford there are dubs or deep pools where the biggest trout lie. With the prospect of just a short day's walk ahead it was possible to idle for an hour along the bank, leaving the fisherman far downstream and finding a muddy outfall where a burn emptied into the river. There were tracks on the water's edge, a confused patter of common sandpipers and mink overprinted by the more measured footprints of a heron. Sorting among boulders in the shallows produced fossil Cycad trunks and fern leaves, and the nymphs and duns of several mayflies. Partridges called from the edge of the wheatfield on the Humshaugh side of the river bend, and there were tufts of forget-me-not all along the banks.

On the north-west side of Chollerford bridge, taking the west road for a few hundred yards, the entrance to Chesters (Cilurnum) Roman Fort appeared on the left.

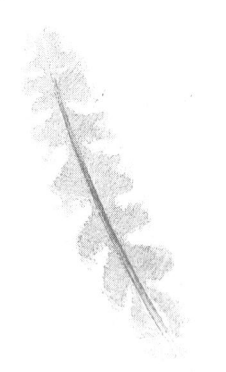

Cilurnum was a cavalry fort guarding the river crossing. The remains of the fort, Wall, baths, settlement and bridge abutments, all in a parkland setting, make Chesters one of the most popular starting places for a tour of the Wall system. It was lucky to find it deserted, even on a chilly morning.

Chesters mansion, hidden among trees on the line of the Vallum to the west, was once the home of John Clayton. Tomlinson's

Partridge feather.

'Comprehensive Guide' of 1888 described Clayton as *'a zealous antiquary, whose good hap it has been to have three of the principal (Roman) stations on his estate, and has thus been able to preserve from the hands of the utilitarian destroyer so many wonderful remnants of Roman power and skill.'* This is certainly true, although modern archaeologists would turn pale at some of the reconstruction work. These days if two stones lie alongside each other they are mapped out and reburied, or bound accurately into place. In Clayton's day they would have been interpreted as a wall, which would then have been rebuilt using any surrounding debris.

The detail of most of the ruins was therefore open to question, and this in turn dampened the impact of seeing such an extensive excavation. The courtyard, next to the headquarters building, was paved with big sandstone blocks. One of these bore a raised carving of a 'lucky' phallus, which must have stubbed many a Dalmatian or Asturian toe. The gates were very clear, as were the heating and drainage systems of the Commandant's House. It was interesting, in a quiet sort of way.

Out of the fort by the lesser east gate, past a clump of yew trees, a path led down to the river and the baths. The Romans enjoyed bathing and made it into a complicated ritual, so it is hardly surprising that some of the most solid and enduring ruins in this cold province are of bath-houses. Chesters bath house is considered to be one of the finest in Britain, but it is just a bath house.

New excavations were in progress at the bridge abutment. A student, clad in anorak and Wellington boots, tee-shirt and shorts, was wheelbarrowing soil from one heap to another, clearing away debris from the original stonework.

Every few centuries the North Tyne has changed its course. Up to 30 million years ago it flowed east to join the Wansbeck rather than south to join the South Tyne. When Hadrian's Wall was first built the river was following its present course, but along a deeper channel over 60 feet further east. A bridge then carried the Wall over the river by a series of arches. In the reign of Severus, early in the third century, the old Wall footbridge was replaced by a more elaborate road bridge, which included a tower, parapets and decorative columns. It is the ruins of this massive structure that now lie exposed on the east side of the river. What was on the west side has been drowned or swept away as the river has eaten into the bank. The work in hand, according to the student, was to sort out what was left. Nothing would stop the North Tyne if it chose to braid a new course.

Clayton's collection of inscribed stones, statues and altars is housed in a building close to the entrance. It hasn't been reorganised since Victorian times, which adds to its attraction as a comment on the life and times of John Clayton but makes it less interesting for visitors in search of history. Five minutes after leaving the museum it was hard to remember anything that had been inside.

To the north-west of the mansion, past stables and by beautiful woodland in which lies a hidden walled herb garden, the Military Road met the line of the Wall again and turned half right, uphill and out of the North Tyne Valley.

A famous nineteenth century engraving shows the foundations of the Wall as part of the road surface as it climbs the hill to Walwick, and the modern asphalt must be no more than a surface skim over Roman rubble. Walwick, a cluster of cottages and farm buildings, overlies a milecastle and spans the Wall and Vallum, but there are no ditches or banks visible as the road jinks from one to the other. On the knoll above the hamlet is a patch of hummocky ground, the site of an old quarry. The dry gorse and bracken was surely hiding more than just a fox earth.

Beyond the farm-yard and hay barn, the views south were of green fields and woodland plantations, the last of the 'civilised' landscape and the start of Northumberland National Park. Beyond Walwick Grange was Warden Hill, on which the Iron Age hill fort still stood out defiantly.

After Tower Tie came a sweep of pasture by Black Carts, with a very clear bank and a long stretch of Wall. A few hawthorn bushes added drama, bent and cowering and sending showers of petals like confetti down the strengthening wind. Following the course of the Wall, the ground rose and the bank to the right fell away until there was nothing to the north but bare fields and the distant parkland around Nunwick Hall and Chipchase Castle. A triangulation column marked the height at 250

Hawthorn flowers.

metres, but it appeared to be much more. This is Limestone Bank, where the Wall turns a corner to pick up the line of the Whin Sill.

Whinstone was extruded into older sandstone sediments nearly 300 million years ago. The magma cooled into a very hard fine-grained rock called dolerite, and this in turn slowly weathered into a distinctive ridge with a steep dip slope facing north. The Whin Sill runs diagonally across North East England, from the Farne Islands to Teesdale and High Cup Nick, but the Romans could only make use of it between here and the River Irthing. It is the landform of the Whin Sill that has turned the Wall into a popular icon and tourist attraction.

To the masons of the Sixth Legion dolerite was a nuisance. It was impossible to dress, and could only be used in construction work as infill; any facings had to be of sandstone. Digging the Wall ditch was a headache too, and at Limestone Bank there were obvious signs that they had started the job but given up. In the ditch, on the brow of the ridge, there were huge boulders with wedge-holes cut into them, still waiting to be split and removed.

On the other side of the Military Road was the Vallum. It ran westwards and was the most obvious landscape feature for miles, narrowing with distance towards Sewingshields Crag. The Vallum mounds were grass-covered but strewn with boulders, and the ditch had been cut through solid rock. In one or two places there were clumps or groves of hazel,

The Vallum, west of Tower Tie. Windswept hawthorn bushes on the edges of the ditch.

growing out of fissures in the rock. Violets and primroses were in flower among the twisted roots. Scrambling down into the ditch was like opening a door into Middle Earth, with a ceiling of dancing leaves, a floor of earth and walls of cold dolerite. With the way ahead nothing more than brightness beyond the green shade of the tunnel, there was a timeless quality to it. Climbing out again into the open broke the spell instantly.

A line of pools ran along the Vallum ditch towards Carrawbrough. One of them contained young palmate newts - small, almost transparent, almost invisible against marsh marigold stems.

Past Carrawbrough Farm and High Teppermoor was the car park for Brocolitia Fort. A pair of crows were pecking at the flattened body of a curlew in the middle of the road. The curlew had probably been run over whilst shepherding its family over to Crook Burn. Crows are well used to traffic; each time a car went past they would hop to the verge, then flap back and carry on for as little or as long as they had before the next car. Crows (corbies) are accomplished scavengers, as efficient as vultures but far more intelligent. They are also predators, stealing the eggs of most waders and game birds. It is only in the last few years (with the increase in grouse management) that their numbers have been controlled. The 'twa corbies' by Brocolitia had checked my skyline silhouette and considered themselves safe.

Brocolitia must have been the worst posting on the Wall. Built much later than the other forts, the Vallum had to be filled in to allow space for it. The name is thought to mean 'Brockholes', originally the site of a badgers' sett, which is quite likely as badgers have always lived in the neighbourhood. There is no record of where the fort's early garrison came from. It was, and remains, a windswept, wet and isolated place.

It was no great surprise to find nothing much there. Brocolitia (or 'Procolitia' as the owner's sign had it) was no more than a raised grassy platform, west of the car park and adjacent to the road. The road

Pheasant feather

Treasure from the molehills of Brocolitia. Fragments of pottery and a hob nail.

still overlaid the Wall. It was possible to trace the fort's gateways and ramparts by pacing the grass-covered ridges and hollows. This soon lost its fascination however; one tuft of grass looked like another and there were no clearer indications. So it came as a shock when a flake of nondescript red stone, picked up from the top of a molehill, resolved itself into a piece of Samian Ware. It was patterned, with a band of what looked like inverted letter '*n*' s. It didn't matter that Samian Ware was mass-produced in Gaul and might turn up anywhere. What did matter was that probably no-one had set hand or eye on this particular piece of pottery for at least 1600 years. It was unique. From that moment on, Brocolitia became a very special place.

Down the slope from the west rampart of the fort was a fence and wall following a marsh southwards. At the head of the marsh was a crumbling fence, around a pool choked by meadowsweet and brook-lime. This marked Coventina's Well. In happier times it was a shrine or wishing well, a place where offerings were made to bring good fortune. When it was excavated in 1876 a total of 13,487 Roman coins were recovered, as well as the altar to Coventina and a host of other 'votive' offerings. They had been among the dusty exhibits at Chesters, overlooked in the hurry to get out into the open air. Seeing the shrine, completely overgrown, brought the words of Maria Hoyer, a visitor in the 1900s, to mind: *"Yes, even the farmers who have used Procolitia as a quarry and laid its walls level with the ground, never dreamt of those thousands of coins so close below their feet! Well done, poor Goddess Coventina, you have been faithful to your trust!"*

Coventina failed in the end to keep the treasure hidden, but that was not what she promised. The real issue was whether she had answered the prayers of all the lovers who had stood gazing at their reflections in her icy waters.

A few yards below the south ramparts stood the remains of the Mithraic Temple, a small building dedicated to the sun god Mithras. It was discovered in 1949 and has been excavated and set out as it would have looked in the fourth century. The three altars that dominate the little temple are replicas; the originals are in the Museum of Antiquities in Newcastle. Because the floor of the building lies below normal ground level it is usually wet, and on this occasion it was awash and would have done justice to Coventina rather than Mithras.

Between the temple and the high grassy ridge of the south rampart, in the area where the vicus or civilian settlement had been, dozens of flattened mole-hills were visible. Having been lucky with the Samian shard there seemed a good chance of finding more pottery in the same way. This time optimism was rewarded, and just half an hour's search turned up a pocketful of treats. The trick was to look around the edges of the mole-hills, where objects had been sifted and washed clean. Among all the stones and bits of field drains there were pieces of Roman glass, a hobnail from a sandal, a broken spindle whorl, and over twenty pieces of pottery. Treasure indeed! It was rich reward for so little effort. Of course most of the pottery fragments were small and plain but, setting them out on a bed of moss, they looked as good as any of Clayton's more famous finds.

John Horsley, in his 'Britannia Romana' of 1733, described a visit to a Roman site where *"pieces of Roman bricks and pots were lying everywhere on the surface of the ground in tillage"*. It came as a surprise to find that this could still be the case, thanks to the local mole population.

The car park had emptied and the crows had picked the curlew clean. A sharp breeze had kept the day cold and the views clear. Poor pasture and barren moorland stretched away as far as the eye can see in every direction. On the horizon to the north was Hedgehope and The Cheviot, 32 miles away, and to the south-west, some 28 miles distant, were Cold Fell and Cross Fell.

A drystone wall provided shelter for a late lunch. But food took second place to rubbing clean the bits of Roman pottery. Cars whined past along the Military Road. Between Brocolitia and the roadside ruin at Shield on the Wall a coach had broken down and the driver was sitting against a wheel, waiting for help. In the pasture alongside was a class of schoolchildren, organised into a circle by their teacher and playing a game. Galloway cattle kept their distance, worried for their blue-grey calves.

Past Shield on the Wall the Whin Sill reared up and the Military road was forced to follow the easier ground to the south. A footpath stayed with the earthworks of the Vallum, whilst the line of the Wall and ditch follows the edge of the Sill. At last the Wall had escaped from the road. Ahead lay some of the most austere and challenging scenery in Britain.

The most imposing feature on the rising ground towards Sewingshields was a sheepfold on the site of a milecastle, which had been planted with sycamores. The trees were geriatric now and their limbs tired, so that a great mop of foliage spread out like an umbrella over the tumbled-down fold. The ditch of the Wall ran close by, and the stones from one merged into the other. Higher up, following the brow of the Sill and stopping at the site of a Wall turret, the wider views carried the eye further afield. To the north, from the foot of the Sill to the dark line on the horizon which marked the start of the Border Forest, lay Haughton Common. A desert of moor-grass covered shallow ripples of sandstone and limestone, and drifted into waves and the high ridge of Hawk Side.

As cloud-shadows rolled over the surface of the Common, the pink of the moor-grass was cast into purple pools, lit by sunshine and shimmering in gusts of wind. In Roman times this was a place of fens and loughs; basins had been scooped out of the rock in the Ice Age, then filled with nutrient-rich water until they were encircled or choked by reeds. When the nutrients were all used up, bog moss covered them over. Only five open loughs have survived into the present century. All of them were visible now, four to the north of the Wall and one, Grindon, to the south.

Wall ditch and sycamores on the side of Sewingshields Milecastle.

The Black Dyke, an Anglo-Saxon boundary, links Halleypike Lough to Grindon. It was easy to trace this shadowy dyke across the landscape to the north of the Wall, but to the south nothing was clear. The soil is shallow on the dip slope of the Sill, and beyond this one sod-cast hedge looked very much like another.

There was a challenge about the Black Dyke, particularly since it led to a beautiful bog called Muckle Moss and a chance to see large heath butterflies. Rather than carry on along the Wall as far as Housesteads, arriving at the fort when it would still be busy with tourists, it seemed suddenly important to be there at a quiet time, perhaps even dawn. The calculations only took a moment and the decision was made; Muckle Moss via the Black Dyke in the late afternoon, Sewingshields Crag and the wilds of Haughton Common for the evening.

Border collies, the working dogs of every hill farm, usually make walking through a farmyard a noisy business. Sewingshields Farm, on the crest of the Whin Sill in the shadow of an arc of tall sycamores, sounded as if it had more than its share of collies. There were at least two in the yard through which the path west was supposed to go. Collies are single-minded when faced with strangers; they circle round and strike silently at heels. The only sure defence is to keep them in front of you, so you end up walking backwards. But with two dogs this was not possible. So instead of striking south from King's Wicket the route became the farm track, meeting the road at the renovated school-house. The field was full of long-haired Galloway cattle, which looked as cuddly as Teddy bears but had a malevolent streak because their calves were about.

The Military road was just as busy as it had been earlier in the day but was quickly crossed. From Moss Kennels a ghost of a path led south, sometimes following an old hawthorn bank which might have been the Black Dyke. Eventually, via Beamwham and with Seldom Seen ahead, the path led out onto the Stanegate road.

The Stanegate was the cutting edge of the Roman Empire in the century before the Wall. Agricola had the road built so that troops could be deployed east or west, based on a series of forts such as Vindolanda and

The old schoolhouse on the roadside at Sewingshields.

Carvoran. It looked modest considering its historical importance; most of it is no longer used as a road and has vanished under grass.

Turning west, the Stanegate took the high ground above Grindon Lough. In the winter there would have been whooper swans and grey-lag geese about the shore, and a peregrine or hen harrier overhead to panic the wigeon. In the middle of summer the water was too low. Past the lough was a small plantation of conifers on the left, and the Black Dyke appeared again to define the boundary. Following the line proved impossible however, because of the marshy ground. Once into the trees everything changed; the wind was still and what had been a background of noise turned to silence, broken only by the explosive rattle of a wren and the wheeze of goldcrests. Cones littered the bare ground beneath the brashed spruces. Red squirrels had stripped all the seeds, and the scales formed a scented carpet.

Trails through the lines of Sitkas narrowed and vanished, and the Black Dyke was lost forever, but after a few minutes of stumbling through the darkness a window of bright sunshine opened to the left. Soon there was heather and bilberry underfoot, and Muckle Moss lay to the south.

Flothers and flows, mosses and mires; Northumbrians have as many names for bogs as Eskimos have for snow. By any standard Muckle Moss is a special place and a permit is usually required to enter. It is a valley mire with heather on its verges and cotton grass and bog-moss at its heart. Beneath the tissue of vegetation lies fifty feet of soaking peat, fed by rainwater collected at the head of Crindledykes.

The upper half of Muckle Moss has always been an open mire but. the lower half was in danger of drying out until the Northumberland Wildlife Trust took over its management. Two post and wire fences run across the valley for a mile separating the holdings. Because the whole bog is fluid and moving downhill, the older fence, initially straight, has bowed and snapped and the replacement is now beginning to do the same. Each year the upper part of the estate gains two or three inches of territory and the bulge in the middle gets more pronounced. The effect is disconcerting. What looks like solid ground is no more than a skin of *Sphagnum* over an ooze of mahogany-brown peat.

Bogs suffer bad reputations; in the case of Muckle Moss it is well deserved. Following its flank and keeping to the heather rather than the more inviting green of the *Sphagnum,* it is possible to reach a willow thicket, from where a narrow roe deer track, well worn and firm underfoot, led straight out over the bog. Somewhere in the middle the roe track passed close by a split in the peat, a black crescent-shaped pool edged by a lip of *Sphagnum* and a ring of cottongrass. Stepping onto the *Sphagnum* just on that spot would have been courting disaster; there would have been no way of scrambling out if the surface had given way. Squatting down and balancing on a hand or elbow was the only way of getting a really close look at the moss cushions. *Andromeda* and cranberry were in full flower among the covering traceries, and there were stems of dwarf willow and asphodel.

The moss cushions proved impossible to sit on even for a moment; although their surfaces seemed dry they behaved like sponges and held gallons of water. It was also impossible to move about. There were sounds of curlews bubbling, then a gentle clatter of dragonfly wings, but there was no way of investigating. A flash of pale tawny-grey wings among the heads of cross-leaved heath could only have been a large heath butterfly. It was on the other side of the peat split and came no closer. After a few moments of hovering around the flower heads, it disappeared down into the clump.

Andromeda, or bog rosemary; a plant of acid bogs.

It was late afternoon and the sun had failed to warm the air. On a sunnier day it might have been worth waiting for roe deer or blackcock, but back at the willow thicket it seemed a better idea to push on west. The Stanegate was only a hundred yards away, reached by beating through a broad bank of heather then turning left onto the road into the weakening light. On the rise was the roadside cottage of Morwood. There was no smoke at the chimney, no tractor in the yard and no dogs. Many years ago, this little cottage must have been an inn, for it was described by William Hutton on his walk in 1801. He called it the Cow and Boot, and took lodgings there after a long day among the stones of Housesteads.

The old man, who described himself as *'the first and probably the last man ever to walk the Wall '*, had been struck by the poverty of local farm workers, and their mistrust of strangers. He appealed to them: *"You must be kind enough to assist me, for there is no other place where I can sleep. Dispose of me how you please, but do not turn me out."* And their response: *"Silence was the answer, which I considered a favourable one. There were, beside the father and mother, six children, chiefly female, and grown up. One of them, a young woman, I was sorry to see, was approaching the grave. Although a public house, they had no ale, cyder, porter, beer, or liquors of any kind, or food, except milk, which was excellent; but they treated me with something preferable, Civility."*

Morwood was grey and silent. All around stretched rushes, bracken and mat-grass; any 'sweetened' fields had been reclaimed by moorland long ago.

Soon Barcombe Fell rose steeply to the left, above the road bearing south towards Bardon Mill. A turning off to the right led back to the Military Road, past an old lime kiln where little owls used to nest. It was too early to think of heading back to the Wall, and Vindolanda was only a few hundred yards away on the other side of the Chineley Burn. Ignoring the contours, the Stanegate headed straight for the fort and its course was visible through the pasture as banks of rushes.

Barcombe Fell invited a climb; on its top there is an Iron Age hill fort, a Roman Signal Station and quarry, but they would have to wait for another day. The slopes were covered in dense heather and in the late afternoon sunshine mountain bumblebees flew to and fro along the banks of bilberry. Half way along the foot of the fell a side-road led down to the right, into the wooded valley of the Chineley Burn at Chesterholm.

Beech trees: smooth grey bark covered with algae and lichens. Beech is a native of southern chalk downs but it has been widely planted in the north and grows well along the Tyne valley.

Large heath butterfly, *Coenonympha tullia*, taking nectar from a flower-head of cross-leaved heath. The size of the black spots on the hindwings varies from colony to colony and there are three recognised subspecies in Britain. The subspecies found in Northumberland is the intermediate form *polydama*.

Bog asphodel. A plant of bogs and wet moorland flushes, growing in dense patches where conditions are right. The flower spikes turn rich saffron in the late summer. After autumn frosts they turn white and papery.

Roosting barn owl. In flight, and in half-light, the plumage looks all white. Close to, the wings and back appear honey-coloured, flecked with grey and brown. Owls look fat, but this is due to feathers rather than flesh and bone.

Primrose among tree roots. In most summers there are a few flowers still out at Whitsun.

Green hairstreak butterfly, *Callophrys rubi*. Colonies of these little green-winged butterflies are found where woodland meets moorland. In Northumberland the eggs are laid on the flowers of bilberry rather than the more usual gorse.

Young fox cat-napping. Foxes often sleep out among the heather and bracken, but in the Wall country they spend a lot of time in the safety of the forest.

Ruby tiger moth, *Phragmatobia fuliginosa*.
The northern form of this beautiful moth is called *borealis*. It has sooty hindwings and flies in June. The adult is on the wing at night and hides among vegetation during the day, but in the spring the furry caterpillar is a common sight along moorland paths.

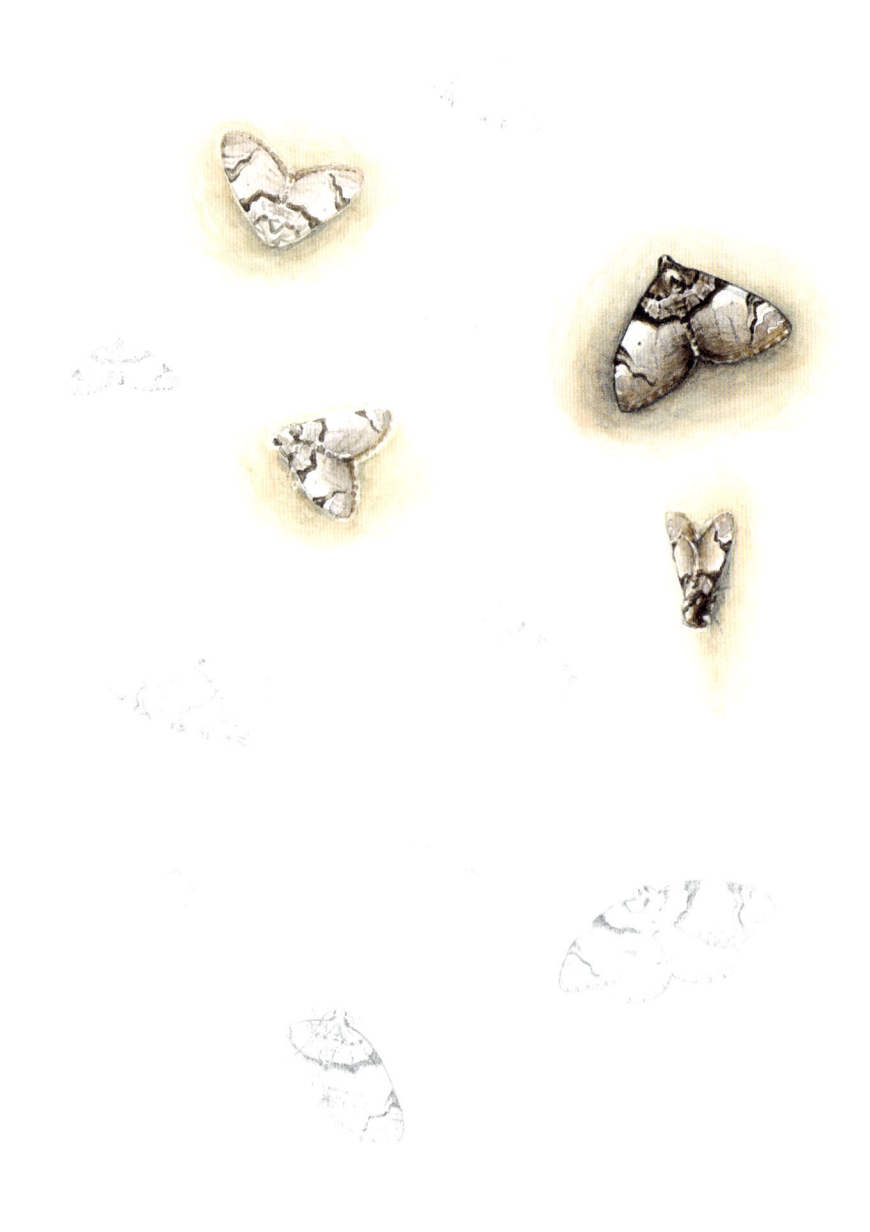

Streamer moth, *Anticlea derivata*.
A geometrid moth of early summer, flying in hedgerows and woodland at twilight. The eggs are laid on dog rose.

Vindolanda would have to wait too; it was closing and people were coming out rather than going in. Vindolanda is the best of all the Roman sites to visit; the interpretation is more friendly and on most days there is something going on, from excavations to re-enactments. Some of the most fascinating information about life on the frontier came from recent digs into the waterlogged soil at the level of the original Stanegate fort. Over 800 writing tablets were unearthed, many indecipherable but some with very readable accounts of day-to-day business. A military report even contained the only known reference to what the Romans called the British; they used the term 'Brittunculi', or 'wretched Britons'. The Stanegate fort was built of wood, of which no trace remains above ground. The visible ruins are from the more elaborate stone version erected around the year 220, as part of the Wall system.

The plateau on which Vindolanda stands is on the west shoulder of the Chineley Burn, above Codley Gate Farm. Opposite the farmhouse is a gate and on the other side of this, in the shade of a spinney of thorn trees, is a Roman milestone. In the first century there were similar five-foot stone markers every mile along the Stanegate, but this is the only one still in its original position.

A path led up the pasture to High Shield and joined the Military Road. Walking east along the road for a few hundred yards there were good views of the Vallum, the Whin Sill and Barcombe Fell. A cock sparrow-hawk, no bigger than a mistle thrush, whipped through a gap in the wall by Bradley Burn and dashed along the verge for a hundred yards, skimming the footings as it tried to flush out pipits or linnets. It was gone in the twinkling of an eye.

The wind dropped with the last hour of daylight. Not far away, was a bank of nettle-covered mounds marking the site of one of the oldest badger colonies in the county. This year's cubs would be half grown and easy to watch around the sett entrance. It took a few minutes to get there, crossing the Vallum and grassy terraces, hoping all the time that the badgers would not be out early, but a hundred yards short of the sett there was a crashing sound and a striped head appeared out of a gap in a forest of bracken fronds.

A boar badger had been rooting in the grass and had only just realised someone was coming. His muzzle was stained with soil. For a full minute he stood stock still; with each second the outline of his head blurred more and more against the vegetation and it was soon hard to tell if he was there at all. Being upwind he could scent nothing, and although something had warned him of potential danger his eyes were too weak to see even a blur. But badgers are prudent by nature; when he moved again it was to turn on his heels and shamble away along a well-worn path.

Sods of earth had been ripped up along the lip of the bank; the badger had been digging for pignuts or bluebell bulbs under the canopy of bracken.

Badger paths often follow eccentric routes, but this one climbed the dip slope straight up to Hadrian's Wall. There was a smudge of ochre on the stonework, marking what was obviously a regular crossing place. Badgers are famous for ignoring obstacles put in their way, from wire fences to motorways. It was tempting to imagine the same thing happening when the Wall was first built, with Brigantian badgers going about their conservative business and treating the barrier as a minor inconvenience.

Housesteads was at its very best. The atmosphere created by the early twilight lent an edge to the scene that would not have been there an hour earlier. The fort was deserted and the only sound came from sheep grazing against the ramparts.

Crindledykes and Bradley north east from Vindolanda.

From a shoulder of whinstone a hundred yards below the south gateway was an all-embracing view of the historic landscape, from the fort on the crest of the Whin Sill down the sweep of the dip slope to the Military Road. In between were grass-covered terraces where the Vallum had been ploughed out in late Roman times to make way for grain crops. In the foreground was the site of the vicus or civilian settlement, in the middle distance was Chapel Hill where shrines to the gods were erected, and to the south-east was the level marshland which must have been the parade-ground. Housesteads, or Vercovicium as it was probably known, was garrisoned by a cohort of Tungrians, from Belgium. They were of

West over the valley of the Chineley burn at Chesterholm, close to Vindolanda.

Celtic origin and must have had more in common with the local British tribes than with neighbouring garrisons.

To reach Haughton Common was the goal, for a view over the moorland in evening light. From Housesteads the Wall ran north-east, crossing the Knag Burn and climbing Kennel Crags. On the banks of the burn were rucks and mounds marking where the bath-house and a lime-kiln lie buried, and nearby was a stone-faced well, overgrown and forgotten.

A brisk walk along the Wall soon led to Sewingshields Crag. The view west from there was particularly dazzling as the sun sank out of the cloud and turned Broomlee Lough into a sheet of fire. There were silhouettes of water-birds on the lough, one of which could have been the red-necked grebe that had recently appeared and would stay for most of the summer.

The Whin Sill at Sewingshields was cast into shadows, broken by columns of dolerite which stood proud of the north-facing cliff and looked like sea-stacks or castle ramparts. Old maps of the Wall even call this place Sewingshields Castle, although no foundations have ever been found and all that exists is a legend about King Arthur and his knights lying in wait in its hidden halls. Further east, through the trees and past the farm, a path slants downhill to the bottom of the scarp and leads north away from the Wall. To the right is Fozy Moss and the sites of a real medieval castle, fishponds and field systems. Nothing was visible now but a sea of purple moor grass.

A track ran between Folly Lake and Halleypike Lough, then north again to the isolated shepherd's cottage at Stell Green. There was nothing at all beyond this; the ground rose in wave after wave of moor grass, disappearing into the gloom. There seemed to be no end to the wilderness.

Another bank of cloud rolled in from the north-west. Vega, the brightest star in the evening sky, shivered and died.

5 Haughton Common - Greenhead

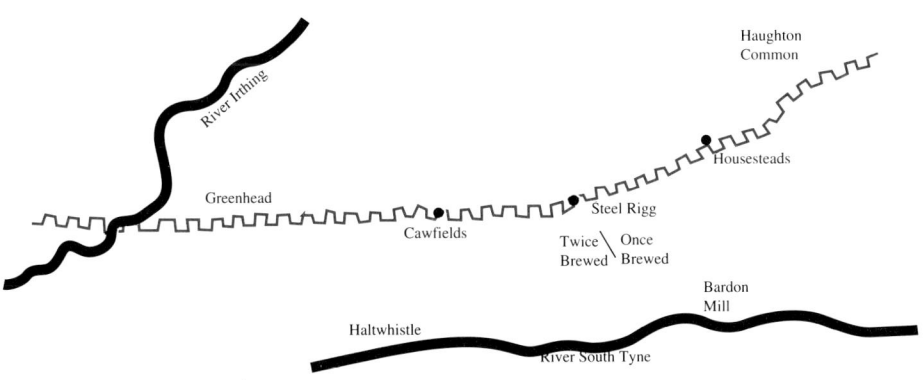

Hawkside - Greenhead: 16 miles

There was nothing romantic about the wilderness at dawn. It was cold, damp and silent.

Across the heather and moor-grass to the north and east ran the edge of the forest, and close to a wall-end on the boundary stood the stone base of Comyn's Cross. Legend has it that a King of Sewingshields Castle, perhaps even Arthur, played host to a travelling knight and sent him on his way in the early morning with a golden chalice. The king's sons were so angry when they heard what their father had done that they rode out and killed the knight to retrieve the chalice.

The Whin Sill and Housesteads Roman Fort, seen from south near Grindon.

Arthurian legends swirl around the Wall country and are no more substantial than the mists over Black Law, but in this case the story may have grown out of a real event. 'Red' Comyn was a pretender to the Scottish throne and his family lived at Tarset Castle in the North Tyne Valley. It seems quite possible that Comyn's Cross marks where one of the family met a violent end, after a raid on Sewingshields during the Anglo-Scottish wars. 'Red' Comyn himself was killed by Robert Bruce at Dumfries in 1307.

On the west side of the open moorland was the steep ridge of Hawk Side. From the top there were views in all directions, south and east over Molinia prairie, north and west over the endless forest. A roebuck grazed a few feet out from the trees, small and roan against the shadows.

The Pennine Way cuts the corner of Haughton Common, heading north towards the Cheviot massif and the Scottish border. The official route goes through treacherous marshland close to a line of shake-holes, where the surface of the ground has collapsed through subsidence in the underlying limestone. A better, drier path runs below the north face of Hawk Side: with a full day ahead it seemed a good idea to start by following the Penine way south, back to the Wall. Moorland soon turned to spruce plantations on the edge of Wark Forest and the Border Forest Park.

There had been no songbirds at all out on the moorland, but into the young plantations there were tree pipits, willow warblers and chaffinches calling. At first it seemed ungracious to bear any grudge against coniferous woodland. There were 'gardens' of spruce saplings clipped and grazed into bonsai shapes by roe deer, and verges of knapweed and melancholy thistle where strengthening sunlight would bring out bumblebees and hoverflies.

The narrow path through new plantings led out onto a metalled drive through mature forest. Tall thin spruces were packed elbow to elbow on either side; their lower stems had not been brashed and they were tangled and tied together, fighting each other for light. There were swathes of windthrow and bare drainage ditches, in row after row like something from the Battle of the Somme. It hardly mattered that there were red squirrels and crossbills in the treetops; this sort of afforestation gives Forest Enterprise (which used to be the Forestry Commission) a bad name. The loss of open moorland seems a high price to pay for woodpulp and chipboard.

The southern edge of the forest had been felled and a new planting strategy adopted, so it was possible to look across less geometric compartments towards Greenlee Lough and the Whin Sill. Watercourses and gullies had been set with rowan and willow saplings; things were changing, and the landscape, if not the moorland wildlife, would benefit in the fullness of time.

What had looked like a flat plain from the Whin Sill turned out to be a series of waves, with alternating bands of sandstone and limestone creating what is called a 'cuesta' landscape. Cutting across the grain of the land emphasised the ridges. After the trough containing Greenlee Lough there was a black heather ridge rising to Queen's Crags, where once there were Roman quarries. Then a sweep of rough pasture before the ground rose to the foot of the Whin Sill. Galloway cattle and Swaledale sheep grazed the outbye. Farms in the Wall country are small; the improved fields immediately around the steading are called the inbye, and the rest is outbye.

For many centuries there were only two breeds of sheep in the Borders. These were the long and the short, of which the long became the Cheviot and the short became the blackface. By the late 19th century other breeds were being developed, of which the most significant locally was the Dishley, which became the Border Leicester. According to a survey of 1803: *"previous to the improvement by the introduction of the Dishley breed the general breed of sheep were called Mugs, a name descriptive of their nature."*

Until a few years ago the normal practice for hill farmers was to cross Cheviot ewes with Border Leicester tups to produce half-bred lambs, or to cross blackface ewes with Border Leicester or Blue-faced Leicester tups to produce Mule lambs. Mule ewes might then be crossed with a Suffolk tup, and the resulting fat lambs would go to Hexham Mart. These days, most flocks are based on Swaledale and the classic breeds of Cheviot and blackface are disappearing, even from the Wall country.

Recent research has suggested that Hadrian's Wall was rendered and whitewashed, so that it would have stood out from miles away. Approaching from the north, along the Pennine Way with the Whin Sill ahead, Housesteads to the left and Hotbank to the right, the Wall hardly showed at all. But glowing white, fifteen feet high and with tall turrets every few hundred yards it would have been a daunting sight. In the troubled times of the fourth century Pictish scouts would have surveyed

Curlew banking into the wind. On the Whin Sill looking south towards the Pennines.

the barrier from this same direction, noted the gaps in the ridge (meltwater channels from the Ice Age) and decided that the Wall was far from impregnable. With the garrisons reduced and the forts half deserted the barbarians must have fancied their chances.

There were several easy ways of getting back onto the crest of the Sill, most obviously by keeping to the Pennine Way and crossing the Wall at Rapishaw Gap. This must have been a well-travelled barbarian route. Lawful traders would have made for the milecastle to the east of Cuddy's Crag, or Housesteads in the next dip along.

East from Cuddy's Crag. A famous view of the Whin Sill and Wall.

We who consider ourselves to live in a civilized country still have a soft spot for the rebels of history. It was a wrench not to follow in the footsteps of the outlaws, and to turn instead along the face of the whin cliff to the security of the milecastle. However, as compensation the scree below the cliffs was worth scanning for plants such as club-moss and parsley fern, and there were wheatears nesting among the fallen columns.

Curlew feathers

Milecastle 37 has been re-excavated in the last few years and is now the best on the whole Wall. The original north gateway, built of great blocks (the hallmark of the Second Legion), had several of the arch-stones or voussoirs in place, and a few paces to the west was the highest standing section of the entire Wall, only two feet less than its full working height.

From below the south gateway of the milecastle the Military Way headed south-west, parallel with the Wall. The Roman track is now grass-covered and forgotten, but firm and dry underfoot and easy to follow. There was no-one about yet and it was still early morning. Somewhere above Bradley Farm and off the top of the ridge there was a clear line separating waterlogged acid soil from more fertile lime-rich ground. On a raised shoulder overlooking the greenest grass was a cluster of hut foundations, dating back to the Bronze Age.

At least four stone circles were visible among the tussocks; it seemed incredible that they had only just been discovered, by a field archaeologist surveying the National Trust estate. A few hundred yards to the west, on the flat lowland by Bradley Burn and very distinct in the low sunlight, ran the enclosure and hut outlines of an Iron Age settlement. When the climate of Britain deteriorated and the crops failed, did the tribe here on the hill move away, and did other tribes or families arrive to establish stock-rearing on the pastures? And had the Romans in turn evicted the Iron Age families from beside the newly dug Vallum? This seems a likely sequence of events.

Bradley Burn (pronounced Braidley) drains the marshland at the foot of Crag Lough, striking south through the Whin Sill at Milking Gap to join Brackies Burn at Vindolanda. On the far side of the Military Road the burn cuts through a gully, and on the rising ground to its left there appear more grass-covered humps and hollows, this time hiding a medieval settlement. The theme seemed worth pursuing.

Sphagnum moss

Bradley Green is the site of a castle, recorded as a stop-over for Edward I on his last campaign against the Scots in 1306-7. It must have been a solid affair, yet no sign of it remains. The most obvious foundations were of bastles or defensible farmhouses of the fifteenth to sixteenth centuries. Perhaps the stone from the castle was used to build the bastles as the community spread and looked to defence against reiving Scots.

What was surprising about Bradley Green was how the medieval farming system had left its mark. There was an enclosing dyke around the settlement to keep stock off the crops, a corn-drying kiln on the bank above the burn, and strip terraces on the slope where the grain was sown. Most clearly of all, there was a sweep in the whole slope which told of generations of one-way ploughing, and a worn shelf between the burn and the cultivated slope where teams of oxen had been drawn back to the start of the circuit.

It was exhilarating and exciting to see 3000 years of history set out across the landscape, not in walls and forts but in fields and farms.

A track led back from the Military Road to Milking Gap. Dozens of trees had been planted in plastic tubes along the Bradley Burn, as a National Park conservation scheme, to link Crag Lough with Chineley Burn and the South Tyne and act as a wildlife corridor. The meadows were coming into flower too, and the sun was out.

Hadrian's Wall crosses Milking Gap close to the foot of Crag Lough. Fen and carr vegetation clothed the shallows, and would one day close in to stifle the lake itself. The Ordnance Survey Map still carries the name of Caw Lough for what is now a marsh towards Greenlee. It is the fate of all the glacial loughs of the Wall country to disappear into fen or carr, then into bog as the nutrients are used up.

Birch trees were the dominant scrub species of the drier carr, as they would have been from the late Stone Age through Roman times to the present day: downy birch *(Betula pubescens)* rather than silver birch *(Betula pendula)*. Some of the trees were dead and rotting, decorated by bracket fungi and witches brooms; birch bark rots much more slowly than the heart-wood, which seems to melt away within a few months. Most trees have entire books written about their traditional uses, but not the birch. William Turner, the 16th century Northumbrian-born herbalist had only this to say on the subject: *"The Frenchmen seethe out of it a certain juice or suc otherwise* called bitumen. I have not read of any virtue that it hath in physic. Howbeit, it serveth for many good uses, and for none better than for beating of stubborn boys."*

The line of the Wall rose quickly westward onto Highshield Crags, with the path on its north side and a steep wooded slope, mostly of pine, hiding the lough below. The Wall itself was missing, having been robbed centuries ago for the building of castles, bastles and farmhouses. When the path came out of the trees there was a breath-taking view down through clefts in the dolerite cliff-face, straight down onto swans, coots and tufted ducks and a sheet of azure-cyanine water. Anyone with vertigo would have backed away in a hurry.

Following the cliff-top path made for slow progress but spectacular views. When this country was in the grip of the Ice Age a frozen sheet of ice several hundred feet thick creaked its way eastwards, scooping out the basins that later became the loughs. When the climate changed the ice began to melt and rivers were formed deep under the frozen surface. These were under such pressure that they cut channels through solid rock. The gaps in the Whin Sill are where the meltwater flowed. The sides are steep so that a walk along the crest of the ridge is a tiring up and down affair.

Two gaps in quick succession separated Highshield from Peel Crags. The first was Sycamore Gap, so called because of the sycamore right in the middle of the cleft. The Wall had recently been consolidated on the slopes and in some places the sandstone was fresh and ochreous. The original mortar still bound the core. When the Wall was first built puddled clay was the rule, but in the extensive rebuild ordered by Severus this was replaced by proper mortar. The distinctive and durable mix of mortar has lasted for eighteen centuries, and in recent years firms such as British Nuclear Fuels have tried to analyse how it was made. Apparently Severan mortar was 60% animal fat, which must have used up a lot of cattle.

On the north side of the Wall close to Sycamore Gap was a swastika, carved by a Roman mason for good luck. It was hard to find and took some searching out, and in the meantime a young couple in red anoraks had clambered up onto the foundations and were keen to see what the fuss was about. They were surprisingly enthusiastic. The girl worked as an usherette in a Glasgow cinema and had promised herself a holiday on Hadrian's Wall, where Kevin Costner had been filmed for 'Robin Hood,

Prince of Thieves'. *"He sat in that tree over there,"* she said. *"I didn't realize it was a real tree."*

The next gap in the whin ridge was Castle Nick, with Milecastle 39, which is one of the best-preserved on the Wall and has been re-excavated over the last few years. Wheatears were nesting among the scatter of boulders on the east slope; the male bobbed and skipped from stone to stone, going further and further away.

The Wall west of Castle Nick, along Peel Crags, ran at shoulder height and was in such a good state of repair that not even clumps of thyme or vernal grass were there to bring it to life. The path beside it was well-worn, showing how popular this famous section has become. Because it was already late morning there were families and couples out walking from the Steel Rigg car park, and beyond Cat Stairs (another cleft in the ridge) climbers were sorting out their gear and anchoring guide-ropes.

At Peel Gap the Wall curves to the south, a deliberate strategy by the builders so that the broad gap could be defended from three sides. It then rises and levels, with a path running along the top of the Wall to meet the road.

The car park to the right was filling up and people were strolling along the path to take in the classic view to the east, but once across the road and up the slope towards Winshields Crags the ridge was deserted again. Winshields is the highest point on the Wall, at about 1,230 feet. Guide books often describe the view as outstanding, taking in Dumfries and the Solway, Cross Fell and Skiddaw. In fact the visibility is usually bad, as it was on this day despite the fitful sunshine.

Crag Lough from Peel Gap.

At the foot of the dip slope on the Military Road are the Once Brewed Youth Hostel and National Park Visitor Centre, and the Twice Brewed pub. The 'Twicey' had recently been painted white after a short but memorable spell of being vibrant yellow. William Hutton stayed at the Twice Brewed on his journey along the Wall. He had found it impossible at first to get a bed to himself; the inn was popular and was full of carriers, *"each with a one-horse cart"*. In fact the Twice Brewed of Hutton's day was not the present large building but what is now called East Twice Brewed, the house along the road.

Looking the other way, north from Winshields Crags, there seemed to be nothing but a few small farms until the start of the Border Forest, with the distinctive radar mast at Hope Alone hidden somewhere in its depth. Again, the terrain is deceptively flattened. Whilst looking towards Saughy Rigg a blur of red appeared and reappeared across ridges and furrows, and eventually a fox came into clear view following the line of a drystone wall. It came on at a steady pace, crossed the wall at a gate and was soon directly below, at the foot of the scarp. It was a large dog-fox, grey around the shoulders and with a well-marked face; a real beauty. The Tynedale Hunt is not the most efficient in the county, and with the advent of the Forest there are more foxes than ever in the Wall country. None of the local farmers can keep hens for very long.

Winshields from Benks Hill. A Roman aqueduct contours the hill on its way to the foot of Aesica.

Having disappeared among the scree it seemed a safe bet that the fox would lie up, but after a few seconds it ambled out again and set off at its earlier pace, retracing its route all the way along the drystone wall. Odd behaviour is a fox's trademark.

West of Winshields the Wall was solid and broad, crossing the gap of Lodhams Slack where the ditch to the north was visible, and following the crest until it disintegrated again into the Bogle Hole and Caw Gap. Another side-road crossed the Whin Sill, but there was no lay-by there and therefore no walkers. Just down the road was Shield on the Wall Farm. This was the second of that name - there had been another at Brocolitia, and there were dozens of other Shields ('Gallowshield', 'Highshield', 'Hangingshield') along the route. A shield or shieling-ground was where cattle were pastured during the summer in medieval times. A rectangular hut became the temporary home of the herdsman, and in the autumn everything was moved back to the safety of the farm. It was during the winter that 'reiving', or rustling by cross-border gangs, turned border life into a bitter fight for survival. Farms evolved into defensible 'bastle-houses' and families learnt swordsmanship. This way of life continued into the eighteenth century, and has left its mark on the land.

East on the Wall at Cawfields Crags.

Cawfields. The Whin Sill has been quarried away to leave a clean cross-section of the ridge.

Cawfields Crags was the next outstanding ridge. The Wall arched and twisted like a serpent along the crest, and the scarp slope was sheer or clothed in aspen and rowan. The terrain was good, the air fresh and the views sparkled. Between the Wall and the Military Road to the south-east ran the line of the Stanegate, a perfect stretch of the Vallum, and a pair of Bronze Age megaliths known as the Mare and Foal. To the south-west, above the Haltwhistle Burn, lay the grass-covered earthworks of a Stanegate fortlet.

Eventually the Whin Sill and Wall descended, past a milecastle to Hole Gap. After this both the Sill and the Wall vanished into Cawfields Quarry. Once, dolerite was widely used for roadstone and several quarries were worked along the Sill. Cawfields, with a lake - indigo-deep and very cold - picnic site and cross-section of the dolerite ridge, had been turned from an ugly sow's ear into a pretty one. Early purple and fragrant orchids, rock-rose and thyme grew on the slabs of worked stone, and heather softened the ledges and corners. It was odd to see rock-rose growing alongside heather; it is supposed to be a calcicole or lime-lover, but in fact it can thrive as long as the soil is basic. Heather cannot tolerate lime, but whinstone (quartz-dolerite) contains no calcium yet is still basic. Hence the association.

Thyme, close-cropped and just into flower.

Stoneflies and mayflies were on the wing along the Caw Burn. It was a mild day with little wind and the promise of afternoon sunshine. Great Chesters Farm, up on the ridge again to the west, still looked cold and exposed and in need of a shelter-belt. Trees have been in short supply in Northumberland since the start of the border troubles; Scottish and English families blamed each other not only for stealing stock but also for cutting down woodland for fuel or building material.

Most of Great Chesters Farm lies on the line of the Wall with its outbuildings to the north, but on its west side is the Roman fort of Aesica. It is on a three acre raised platform, covered with grass except for the turrets and central strong-room, and it has an air of secrecy about it, of quiet contempt for whatever is going on in the world. A hoard of beautiful Celtic jewellry was dug up from the west tower of the south gate a century ago. More recently a milecastle site was discovered on the original Broad Wall and partly underlying the fort; the Narrow Wall was not built on existing broad foundations as at other forts but was built alongside it to the south, so the redundant milecastle with its gateway would not be a weak point in the defences.

There were no signs or panels to gild the lily. Aesica relied for its impact either on prior knowledge or a vivid imagination. It was the same when Hutton was there in 1801: *"The appearance of the place, and the idea of past transactions, strike the soul with awe,"* he wrote. As with most of

Altar stone and south gateway, Aesica.

The West Gate and wall of Aesica.

South-west turret, full of nettles.

Aesica strongroom; built to last.

N ←

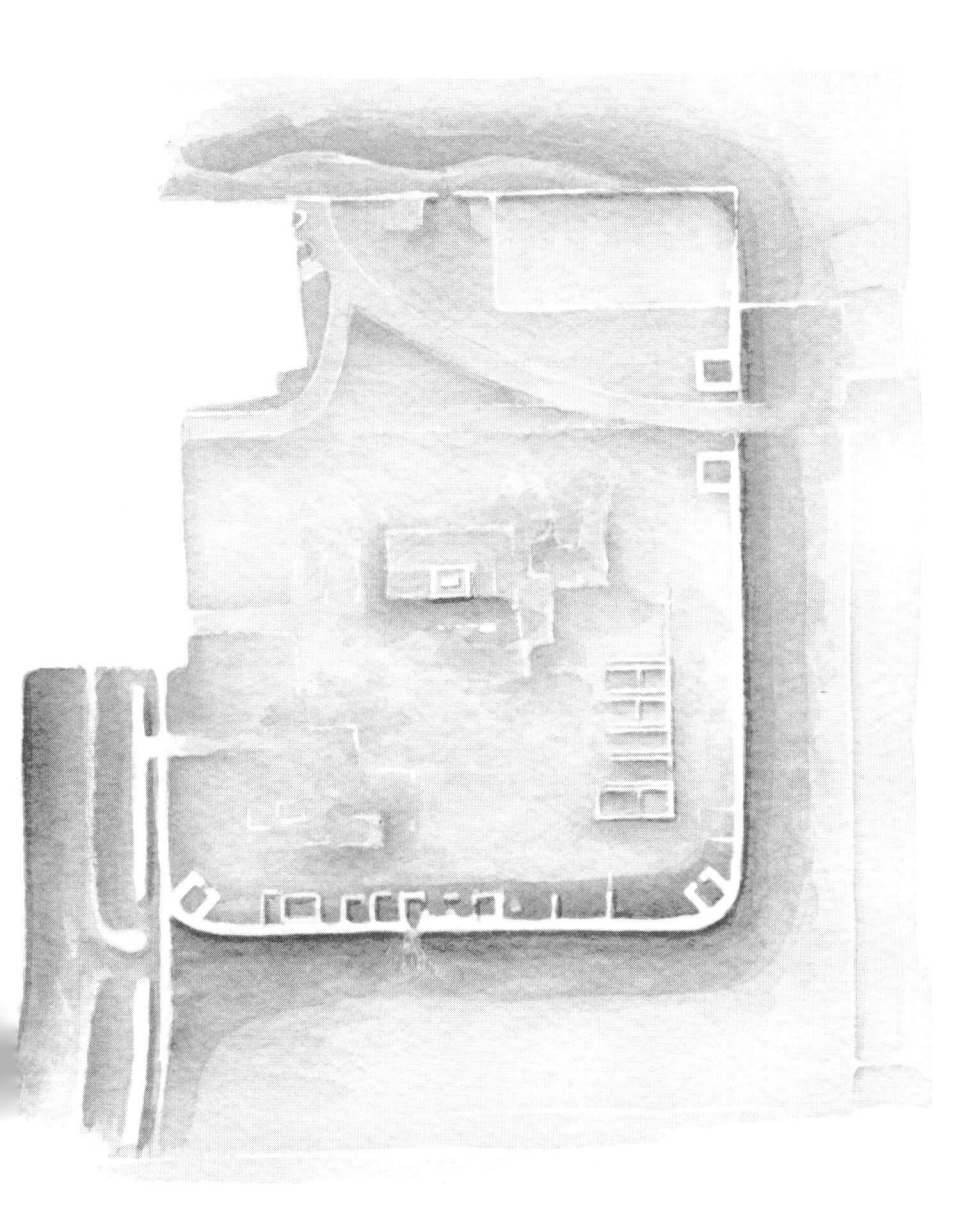

*Great Chesters; plan of the visible remains of Aesica Roman Fort.
Grass covers most of the ruins, which lie to the west of the farm.*

the Wall forts, the setting is everything. The prospect of the ridge at Cockmount Hill to the west was spectacular and the open country to the north wild and wind-swept. From the scarp edge below the north-west tower it was just possible (with a little imagination) to pick out the wandering line of the aqueduct which carried water to the fort from Swallow Crags. The channel contours around the Caw and Pont Gallons Burns for six miles to reach the fort; the direct line would have been little over two but the Roman engineers wanted to avoid having to build too many bridges or embankments.

The little farm-steading on Cockmount Hill was backed by trees and had a great sweep of a view to the south and east, but its immediate surroundings were spartan. For years the house has lain empty. Walking past the front windows was an uncomfortable business, but the unblinking stare came not from the house but from a young merlin sitting on the paddock wall outside. At first it sat half-crouched and the line of its tail, rump, back and nape were a natural extension of the stone. Only its head moved, to keep both beady eyes on the passing danger.

Merlins, unlike kestrels, don't nest along the Wall and it is easy in the

Merlins

excitement of the moment to mistake one falcon for another. And where peregrines, goshawks and kites are increasing in numbers, merlins have been declining for the past few years; the reason may be the loss of moorland habitat or an indirect effect of pesticides. But there are still healthy breeding populations in the North Pennines, and it is a short flight from Cold Fell over the Tyne Gap to the Whin Sill. Last-year's youngsters would have ranged widely in their search for territories. This one looked to be a male, small and showing grey among the chocolate-brown of its plumage. It was wary and quick to be away. One moment it was part of the wall, the next it had flown. It only appeared above the skyline again when it was several hundred yards to the east, no more than a dark arrow following the contours of the Wall. Somewhere towards Aesica it was spotted by jackdaws and there was a cackling of angry voices as they tried to bully it on its way.

Cockmount probably got its name from being a haunt of woodcocks, and the block of damp woodland west of the farm, above the Vallum and the marshland of the Loddams, must still be prime habitat. Along the path there was a scatter of feathers where one had been killed, and every few paces there was a familiar acrid musky scent of fox.

Woodcock

Out onto the open crest of the Sill again, the Wall was sometimes several courses thick and sometimes a pile of rubble. It veered north-west to the site of Allolee milecastle, then climbed higher and higher and angled south-west to follow an impressive dog-toothed ridge towards Walltown. This run of high crags and deep gaps is still called the Nine Nicks of Thirlwall, even though Walltown Quarry has eaten away most of its western end.

Woodcock feather

What had been the most exhilarating stretch of the Wall also threatened to be the most tiring, and after a couple of stiff down-and-ups to Mucklebank Crag it was hard to retain the interest in the passing landscape or its history.

West towards Walltown Crags and turret.

Walltown turret provided both an excuse and an incentive to stop. It stands on the western end of Muckle Bank with a steep drop down to Walltown Nick, where the Wall does an inward arc as another defensive 'enfilade'. There were limitless views all around, and because the air had cleared through the day the Solway coast shone like molten bronze. The turret was at a sharp angle in the Wall with a good prospect to the west; garrison soldiers would have enjoyed some beautiful sunsets and had early notice of storms.

At the foot of Walltown Nick lay a marsh, with a well sunk into the spring-line beside the Wall. This is known as King Arthur's Well, one more reference to the legendary British king who resisted the Saxon invasion during the Dark Ages.

Walltown was once a village with a tower-house. The stone for the present farm must have come from the castellated tower, which would in turn have been built from Wall stone. Most of the cottages and long-houses in the lost village would have been built of wattle and daub; mud or mortar on a framework of sticks.

In the sixteenth century a Luddite called Harrison linked improved housing with the decadence of his age: *"When oure houses were buylded of willowe, then had we oken men, but now that our houses are come to be made of oke, our men are not only become willowe, but a great many altogether of straw..."* He also lamented the passing of open wood-burning fires and the introduction of coal: *"Now we have manye chimneys, and yet our tenderlings complaine of reumes, catarres, and posses; then had we none but reredosses, and our heades did never ake."*

Life at Walltown would have been hard, with or without coal. When William Hutton passed the door of Walltown Farm there were Roman altars on either side, one of which had *"at last the honour of supporting the dish-clout ... I saw one old female, who treated me shily, and heard a younger, who durst not see me; and both, I have reason to think, wished me gone."* Hutton climbed the slope up to the turret remarking that William Camden (a 16th century antiquary) *"was terrified.... at the imaginary houses of the Moss Troopers, and relinquished his examination of the Wall..... I found the ascent so difficult that I sometimes was obliged to crawl on all fours."*

The descent was tricky too. Half way down, following the residue of the Wall, a boulder bounced past and crashed into the scree at the bottom. Luckily there was nobody about.

On the broad dip slope of the ridge there were patches of dolerite where the soil is wafer thin or missing altogether. These hard plates of rock, still showing scratch-marks from glaciers, were edged with all the characteristic whin flowers, such as parsley piert and rock rose. There were also patches of wild chive, the plant the Romans are supposed to have introduced as a herb. Every patch had been cropped by discerning sheep, leaving no flowers.

Walltown Crags were the reprise of the Whin Sill and the Romans had done them full justice, shadowing the cliff edge with the Wall. Turret 45a doubled as a signal station, and the views are correspondingly good. Nearby in the dips the Wall is ten feet high and in prime condition, but heavily consolidated.

Everything came to an abrupt end at Walltown Quarry. The grassland, the cliff, the path, the Wall; everything. The quarry had been much bigger and more damaging than the one at Cawfields. When it closed it left an open sore, which is only now healing into a grassy picnic site. Having to turn down to the road and skirt the workings was frustrating. There was at least some consolation in the new wildlife habitats created by the reclamation work; it was good to hear willow warblers and whitethroats singing from the thickets and see a common blue butterfly settling down to roost on the grass stems beside the quarry gate, but it still made a sad end to the most spectacular stretch of the walk. A few years ago, there was talk of turning the quarry into a Hadrian's Wall Theme Park, with a full reconstruction of a section of Wall; thankfully nothing further has been heard of this.

Hadrian's Wall, showing careful stone-laying, on the hill slope at Walltown.

Where the Whin Sill ended there was still high ground to carry the line of the Wall west, above the Museum of the Roman Army and the site of the Stanegate fort at Carvoran. The Wall itself went missing again, having been used to build Thirlwall Castle. An ordinary drystone wall traced its path, with a very clear ditch alongside it until a walled track zigzagged down through woodland to Holmhead Farm. Dogs barked, washing danced on the line, and there was a farm-mix of smells of wood-smoke, slurry and diesel. The only people about were two small children, who were playing with pebbles on the banks of the Tipalt Burn below Duffenfoot. The game looked very complicated and absorbing, the children squatting among a semi-circle of farmyard ducks, daubing water-patterns onto stones and sifting dry silt through their fingers.

The Tipalt drains the mires of Thirlwall Common and is stained by the peat, either Venetian red or mahogany depending on the season. On this day the water was quite dark; the rain of the previous week had been absorbed into the bog-moss and not yet found its way into the sikes and streams.

The ruins of Thirlwall Castle teeter on a spur high above the gorge. A footbridge crossed the burn just downstream of where the children had been playing and there is a sheep path up from Duffenfoot to the crumbling tower. Thirlwall was another stopping place for Edward I, in the autumn of 1306 and before his last campaign. The castle must have been new then, but it is hard to believe it could have been very comfortable. What remains is falling to pieces, eaten away like a rotten apple so that the massive walls overhang the steep slope and piles of masonry lie where they have fallen. A kestrel called overhead, hidden by saplings growing out of the rubble. There was a nest high on the west wall, marked by lime-splashes and fragments of dead prey.

Thirlwell was made out of Roman stone and there are dog-toothed facings from the Wall lying at the foot of the bank. A splinter from a broken stone became another souvenir, joining pottery shards and four-leaved clovers in the treasure trove.

The washing had gone from the line at Holmhead. A path leads from Duffenfoot downstream on the opposite bank, away from the castle and onto the wide flat pasture between the Tipalt and the Pow Charney Burn. The Wall had stood on this point, straight and level and at its most vulnerable. The name 'Thirlwall' is supposed to refer to the breaching (or 'thirling') of the Wall by Caledonians or Barbarians. No trace of Wall, ditch, military road or Vallum remains. For once, there was not even a hedge to mark the limits of the Empire.

Northern eggar moth.

6 Greenhead - Carlisle

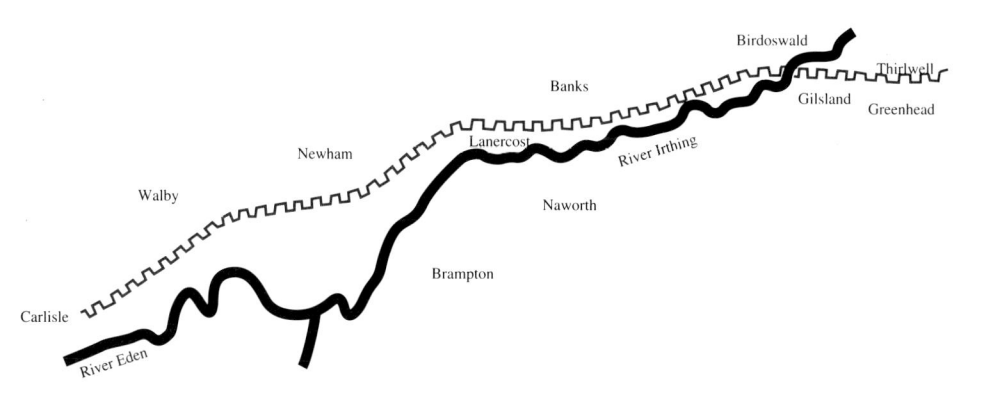

Greenhead - Carlisle: 17 miles

Sun and rain had washed the early morning oyster-grey light from the sky by the time Greenhead was awake; there were no sounds until stray shafts of sunshine struck the tower of St Cuthbert's Church and set the jackdaws chattering.

The A69 used to run through the middle of Greenhead but a by-pass has brought peace to the village. The hotel and garage must have rued the day however, losing the custom of road travellers. The subsequent increase in walkers along the Wall and the Pennine Way will have been no compensation; walkers are not known for the generous custom they bring. Mars bars and a bed at the Youth Hostel would be the order of the day.

In the middle of the village, beside the church, stood an ornate Victorian fountain dedicated to the memory of John Blenkinsop Coulson. Blenkinsopp, with the extra 'p' on O.S. maps, will be more widely remembered by walkers as the name of a plateau of moorland to the south called Blenkinsopp Common. This sodden waste comes at the end of a long section of the Pennine Way and is hard to forget. Long ago the fountain ceased to flow and the basins were filled with soil and bedding plants. In the dour Wall country such touches of green are welcome, so perhaps Mr Coulson would have been happy with his memorial.

The River Irthing marks the natural boundary between Northumberland and Cumbria, so the scrap of Cumbria between Greenhead and Gilsland is a curiosity. Three Roman camps, at Glenwhelt Leazes, Chapel Rigg and Crooks, lie on spurs of moorland overlooking the line of the Stanegate and the Wall at this point, and there are forts on either side at Carvoran and Birdoswald. Clearly, this was a weakness in the chain where the terrain favoured the enemy to the north. It was just above Greenhead, on the levels beside the Tipalt Burn, that the Wall was breached in the Barbarian Conspiracy of 367 when a combined attack by Picts, Scots, Saxons, Franks and Atocotti easily over-ran the defences and threatened to wrest Britain from the Empire. It took one of Rome's finest commanders, Count Theodosius, to sort things out.

With the whole day ahead, and the morning in which to reach Birdoswald, it was safe to wander off the course of the Wall. In any case, there are no visible remains until the Poltross Burn milecastle at Gilsland. The first detour was to a farm outbuilding a little way from the village where barn owls had once roosted. Thirty years ago the barn owl was the most likely of owls to see around the countryside, taken for granted by farmer and naturalist alike.

It was not until it had gone that anyone realized it was at risk. Loss of traditional farmland and breeding sites in old barns was eventually

Barn owl

blamed. The open moorland of the North Pennines is short-eared owl country and was never suitable for barn owls, yet on this spot a pair was always to be found.

Brushing past the cobwebs and entering the crumbling outbuilding was like walking into a church, full of hushed silence and shadows. After a few seconds the blackness eased and a pale stump on a brick buttress defined itself into the solid outline of a sleeping owl. It was a brief and unexpected encounter, which is so often the way with birds. The white owl's eyes were half open, watching like a sleeping cat. For an instant its body seemed to tense and shrink, the plumage drawn in as a prelude to flight, but it stayed and held its ground, and it was possible to back away to the door without breaking the spell. Outside again, breathless and tense, it felt as if hours, not just a few seconds, had passed.

North of Thirlwall, and bearing north-west as the Tipalt turned north-east, a path by the Pow Charnley Burn and along the county boundary led at last to the Irthing. This is one of the most difficult of rivers to follow, sinuous and steep-sided and with few paths to find a way. Upstream of Collering Wood lie desolate miles of forest and bog. The forest looks pretty from afar but is monotonous and dreary. With bogs it is the other way round; the emptiness is frightening but in detail the flora and fauna is dazzling.

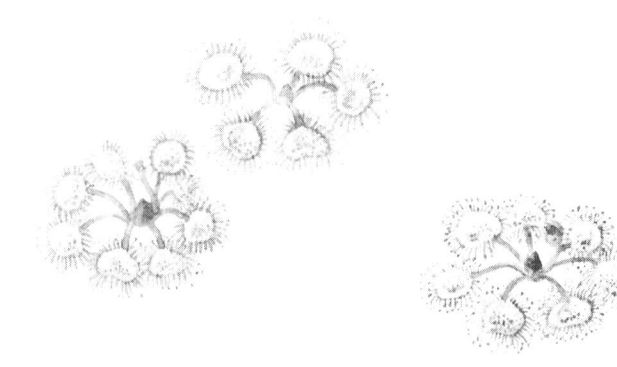

Sundews growing among the bog moss.

The Irthinghead mires are famous among those who appreciate peatlands; unfortunately some of the best areas were drained and planted by the Forestry Commission, and on the Cumbrian side the great sweeps of wilderness lie within Ministry of Defence territory on the Spadeadam Ranges.

Upstream and downstream of Gilsland the Irthing cuts through beds of sandstone and limestone, creating cliffs and wooded gorges of such beauty that it is difficult to see how it has remained such a secret.

By Wardrew a badger path led down into the bower of woodland. The maiden trees on the slopes are oak, ash and sycamore; sycamore comprising more and more of the canopy having competed and won space from the natives. Close to the river are striplings of sallow, alder

Maiden oak; in a hedge near Gilsland.

The Irthing Gorge. An inspiring sight, and it may have been where a British army (led by a warlord who may have been Arthur) lost the vital battle against the Saxons.

and bird cherry. Although there had been rain over the last few days the river was quiet and low. It was easy to tip-toe across slabs and shelves of honey-coloured stone to the west bank where there were standing pools of peat-stained water. Bathed in translucent shade, the deepest pools were like polished mahogany, reflecting green to green. It was hard to know where water and stone turned to air and foliage. Upstream, sandstone cliffs rose vertically on the east bank and there were shoots and cascades of water bouncing light and sound across the gorge.

Bird cherry

For some time there was no song or movement from any of the woodland birds that must have been nesting nearby. Then one after another they appeared, drawn from cover by the harvest of water-borne black Simuliid flies. Spotted flycatchers were especially obvious, perhaps a family of parents and full-grown young, each bird in a different oak tree. From a lookout branch one or other launched itself down over the bank, fluttering and hovering for a few seconds to snap at the flies before returning to the same perch. Among the hazel and alder bushes there was a cock redstart, tail flicking and quivering at each hop and bounce, from bush to stones and back again. The female came out just for a few seconds, less inclined to leave the shadows but hungry and with a family to feed. Willow and wood warblers, blackcaps and a single pied flycatcher made up the assembly.

One of the shallower pools was full of tadpoles. Whilst looking into the pool the patch of sky reflected in the water was sheered in two by the silhouette of a bird of prey; the eyes of every small bird must have turned skyward at the same instant. It was a peregrine, a tiercel carrying prey, beating northwards to an eyrie on MoD land. Had it been free of its burden it would have vanished in an instant, no sooner seen than lost.

From the enclosed world of the Irthing another badger path led up through beds of bluebells to join the footpath and the road by Common House. Gilsland, and the Wall, lay less than a mile to the south.

The milecastle at Poltross Burn was too close to the railway line for comfort. To the west of this however, and accessible from the same side-road and close to Gilsland School, was a fine stretch of Wall leading towards Willowford Farm.

It was playtime at the school and a crowd of children had gathered next to the railings. They were watching a roadworker who had stopped for a cup of tea and was sitting on an oil drum a few feet away. The man looked uncomfortable; one weathered hand held a mug and the other, hidden from the children behind his back, held a cigarette. The audience clearly didn't approve and he was happy to break the tension and bid good morning to a passer-by. *"Not many people bother with the Wall,"* he commented. *"Too much television."*

From the road the Wall ran north-west with the contour, the valley slope to the right and a meadow full of brome grass and clover to the left. After the farm it fell quickly south-west to meet the river as it twists back on itself.

The ruins of the Wall, clearer here than for several miles, were on broad ten foot foundations, the prescription by which Hadrian's plans were set. By the time the legions had built the turrets, milecastles and foundations the regulations had changed, and the upper courses were completed to a narrower gauge. Hence some odd sections of Wall between Poltross Burn and the abutment. The Irthing is where the broad foundation comes to an end; a shortage of lime (for mortar) forced the Romans to use turf rather than stone all the way to Bowness. Although the Sixth Legion quickly replaced the crumbling turf with stone for the five miles west of Willowford this was of the narrow gauge, on narrow foundations.

At the bottom of the hill, and having run straight as a die down from the farm, the Wall ended not at the river but in the middle of a field. This seemed odd at first; it is not common to see a landscape change - it is usually the human influences that come and go. What had happened was that the force of the river had been concentrated since the Ice Age on the outer sweep of the bend and this had eaten away the west bank. The build up of silt on the inner side had filled and levelled the old river. There were no clues where the river had been to begin with; presumably at the foot of the slope below the farm, but the remains of the Wall, tower and abutments showed exactly where it was by the second century.

There were no willows at Willowford, and no bridge to cross the Irthing. Rather than have to go all the way back into Gilsland and cross by the B6318 it seemed a good idea to wade the shallows. This was not as easy as it looked, even in bare feet; half way across there was a channel where the current pulled and starbursts of reflected light did their best to hide the boulders.

Climbing the wooded west bank of the Irthing, circling to the south to find a path and following this up to Harrow's Scar, the view to the east opened out to the Nine Nicks and the Whin Sill, which had been left behind across the Northumberland border. The milecastle on the hill-top overlooks the Irthing but trees hide most of the lower valley and there is only a narrow gap through which the Wall can be seen. Around the milecastle cattle had poached and churned the ground and were standing shoulder to shoulder barring the only path. They responded slowly, and even then it took threats and gestures and they only shifted their ground a few feet. Perhaps they were used to tourists. Both the milecastle and Wall were in good condition, high and consolidated so that the facings looked new. Close-cropped pasture ran ahead all the way to Birdoswald Fort. The Wall at last had become a frontier, blocking the view to the north and leading away into the distant west.

Post-hole from the East Gate at Birdoswald Roman Fort. Well-worn, and therefore well-used.

Two surprises made Birdoswald special. The first was the Turf Wall, the short-lived continuation of the Wall from the Irthing to Bowness. In most places there is nothing left of this feature because the Stone Wall was built along the same line, but on either side of Birdoswald the Turf Wall runs to the south and is sometimes visible as a ridge. On the approach from the east beyond Harrow's Scar it is more of a ghost than a reality, but there would be no fun in a Wall walk without imagination and there certainly seemed to be the hint of a ridge running parallel with the Stone Wall and striking the side of the fort close to the east gate. In fact the line of the Turf Wall runs straight through the fort, because the fort was not part of the original defences. Although no more than a vague ridge it was exciting and mysterious in a way that the nearby stonework was not.

At the fort, through the farmhouse that has recently been turned into a modest Visitor Centre, the second surprise was the young information assistant at the till. Flaxen-haired and fired with enthusiasm, she transformed a handful of dry questions into a guided tour. This turned out to be an unexpected treat; she was new in the job and keen to impart her knowledge. After skipping from the Roman graffiti on the Wall to the recent excavations in the fort itself she led the way back to the farmhouse across a dark smudge on the cleared ground; the smudge turned out to be the Turf Wall. What had once been a mound twenty feet wide and up to sixteen feet high had been reduced to a veneer of peat.

Roman graffiti on the Wall just east of Birdoswald Fort; phallus and cross.

The tour ended gazing out over Midgeholme Moss, following the line of the Roman Road towards the outpost fort at Bewcastle. (A system of outpost forts had been established in the days of Hadrian, but Count Theodosius had had them dismantled after the Barbarian Conspiracy.)

Birdoswald, known to the Romans as Banna, was built on top of an Iron Age settlement and was intended to defend the Willowford crossing. The fort commands the highest ground on a bluff overlooking the Irthing, and

The Wall from Birdoswald towards Willowford.

from the south gate it is a stones-throw to the edge of the gorge. This was the ideal place to settle for lunch and to paint the landscape below. A canopy of trees swept down to the river; jays and wood pigeons flapped across the gap and for an instant a sparrow-hawk stitched a thread of panic through territories of songbirds. The scene was timeless, perfect but for an icy wind, watercolour that wouldn't dry, and the feeling that the day was half spent and not a quarter walked.

At first the road west of Birdoswald ran beside a good stretch of Stone Wall, but beyond a turret this ended and there was nothing but the fighting ditch to mark its progress. Across the field to the south was a very clear stretch of Vallum and a proper section of the Turf Wall. Once past Wall Burn the two lines met again and the Turf Wall disappeared

By-road north of Wall Bowers.

into history. The view to the south was of the Irthing Valley again, just as beautiful. On the far side of the river lay the site of Nether Denton Fort, built by Agricola and guarding the Stanegate in the years before the Wall. A church and rectory now stood on the spot.

West again and the road passed two turrets on the left and Leahill Farm on the right before arriving at a car park beside a section of Wall and another turret. This was Banks East. Two cars were on the tarmac, both with people inside sheltering from the stiff breeze. Nobody was looking at the turret; the main attraction seemed to be the view of the North Pennines. A short footpath led back parallel to the road to the Roman signal tower at Pike Hill. Again, a little mystery added spice to this feature, for although it had been spoilt by road-building in the last century it was possible to imagine its purpose as a high tower for distant signalling. By scrambling down the grassy bank below the tower, among the hawthorns, it was easy to get out of the wind, away from people, and see the best of the landscape. The enclosed pastures and hedges of the valley petered out in the distance and the North Pennines were laid bare. Cold Fell and its sisters lay smouldering in grey cloud.

At the hamlet of Banks there was a choice of routes and a dilemma. The line of the Wall continues due west over Craggle Hill, away from the road and therefore an attractive prospect. But hidden down the road lay Lanercost Priory, one of the most beautiful buildings in the North of England. The answer was to miss nothing by detouring to Lanercost and

Banks turret.

returning up the road to Banks. This proved a wise move; the sun broke through and for half an hour the countryside was awash with vibrant colour.

There can be few places so English as the square mile around Lanercost Bridge. Naworth Castle, home of the Howard family and the Earls of Carlisle, lies across the parkland to the south. A dozen woods, the Irthing and its feeder becks and gills, the Augustinian Priory in a patchwork of meadows and pastures; all these lie between the Stanegate and the Wall. It is the sort of landscape that is supposed to have been swept away with the Great War.

Swifts circled the priory tower, one minute high and lost in the sky, the next spiralling into screaming packs and chasing each other over the cloisters. Perhaps they nested in those same eaves in the twelfth century when the Priory was built. What would the canons have made of such strange 'devil birds'? They would never have believed what we now know; that swifts spend most of their lives on the wing, fly thousands of miles over oceans and deserts, never touch the ground, sleep, eat and mate in flight and return each year to the same high crevice in which to lay their eggs.

Lanercost Priory is a ruin built from a ruin. Its red sandstone comes from the Wall and must have taken all the facing stone for miles. The building manages to combine solidity with grace and elegance. Medieval tombs, Roman inscriptions and ruined vaults are visible, with just enough information to interest the visitor. The Priory was built by the Vaux family in the late 1160s. After a prosperous thirteenth century the Anglo-Scottish wars brought disaster in the form of William Wallace, Robert Bruce and other vengeful armies.

King Edward 1 stayed here on several occasions. The Chronicle of Lanercost records one of the visits: *"...on the third of the ides of September my lord King of England and his queen Eleanor came to Lanercost, and the prior and convent met them at the gate in their capes. ....the king presented a silken robe, and the king in his hunting took, as was said, two hundred stags and hinds in Inglewood."* It says a great deal about how the Hammer of the Scots whiled away his time between wars. There are no red deer now in the woods of north Cumbria.

The life of the Priory came to an end with the Dissolution of the Monasteries in 1539. Lanercost was granted to the Dacre family, who lived there before moving to Naworth. In the reign of Elizabeth I it was to Lord Dacre that the Earls of Northumberland and Westmorland turned for sanctuary following their failed rebellion and defeat at Geltdale. With a pitiful band of refugees they made for Liddesdale across the border, but on the way they called in desperation at what was described by William Armstrong as *"the one house ... where, if anywhere in England, rest and shelter could not honourably be denied them. This was Naworth Castle, the home of their recent confederate, Leonard Dacre."* Unfortunately Lord Dacre was more concerned with life than loyalty and the rebels were turned away.

Back in the courtyard there was a notice warning drivers that the cows eat car aerials. Cattle were all around, looking casual, and the adjacent holding pens were full of sheep waiting to be sheared.

The walk back up the road to Bank Foot and the track west to follow the line of the Wall took only a few minutes but in that time the sun sank into a leaden bank of cloud. Rain was in the air. At Hare Hill there was a short fragment of Wall, over ten feet tall and therefore of special note, but most of the facing stone in the seventeen courses were added in the last century. The north side carried a centurial stone, inscribed <P.P., meaning the stretch of Wall had been built by the century of men under the Primus Pilus (Chief Centurion of the Legion). This stone too had been re-located, but it looked well enough. The Wall was eight feet wide, the 'Intermediate' size used for the last replacement of the Turf Wall. Hadrian's successor Antoninus Pius established a new boundary for the Empire across the Clyde-Forth isthmus, but this was abandoned and the old frontier re-established around 190 AD.

The next mile was exciting. There were no waymarks and no path at all, and flurries of rain swept across the rolling hills ahead. Craggle Hill had been cropped for silage; rooks covered the fields to left and right, swaggering about like clowns in baggy black trousers. To the right of the old sod-cast dyke, marking the line of the Wall, there was a very distinct and deep section of the ditch. This was full of rushes and ferns,

Centurial stone inscribed by the mark of the Primus Pilus, at Hare Hill.

buttercups, bluebells and lady's smock. The hedge on the sod-cast was hawthorn and blackthorn, with majestic sessile oaks. Tufts of lady's mantle grew on the better drained soil. Past the ruins of Haytongate Farm, and over a footbridge spanning Burtholme Beck, the sod-cast suddenly turned into the Wall and there was a stretch of about 36 yards of wonderfully crumbling rubble. This was not the carefully conserved DoE version but the original untouched masterpiece,

The Wall ditch on Craggle Hill.

Lady's mantle

lacking most of its facing stones and shattered into a thousand pieces by tree roots. Of all the Wall along the entire 73 miles, this was undoubtedly the most inspiring.

This path seemed to have been forgotten; the grass was untrodden and the way unmarked. For a second it was possible to see with the eyes of William Hutton.

Plantations of pine and spruce lay to the left, and Walton Wood a hundred yards to the right. The ditch was still very obvious, but over the rise of the next hill, below Garthside, the marshy ground spread out right across the pasture. For a few hundred yards the Stone Wall was supposed to leave the line of the Turf Wall, encouraging more speculation. There were several ridges and possible ditches, and some stones break the surface, but it was impossible from the signs to sort anything out. Apparently there had been two turrets on the lee of the hill; the first, with its original ditch, had been built of clay, and a replacement had been built of turf. Eventually the Stone Wall was built over the top and the turrets were obsolete. None of this could be read from the surface, even with the help of a vivid imagination.

With the passing of the rain there seemed to be confetti in the air; the lady's smock had attracted green-veined white butterflies and there were eight or ten together, pirouetting and tumbling in mating flights over the banks of flowers. Green-veined whites are the most widespread of British butterflies, often mistaken for 'cabbage whites' but with distinctive green dusting around the veins of the underwing. The caterpillars feed on crucifers such as hedge garlic and lady's smock rather than cabbages.

Thirty or forty years ago, this would have been the time and place to expect a dozen species of butter-flies, such as the pearl-bordered and small pearl-bordered fritillaries, but now not enough flower-rich habitat is left to sustain them.

Past the side-road to Walton and following no obvious features, the line of the Wall headed across fields and past Howgill Farm, where there was an inscribed stone built into an outhouse. Westward again it lost height, off the shoulder of the ridge, and crossed the King Water at Dovecote Bridge. Just past the pretty bridge and to the right of the road was the last surviving section of Roman stones. From here to Bowness there would only be clues in the landscape to suggest there had ever been a Wall.

Walton had all the essentials of a Cumbrian village except for a noisy road. The settlement grew up around a church and crossroad, but over the years travellers took easier routes and neither the roads nor the village grew. St Mary's Church stood on twelfth century foundations but was rebuilt in red sandstone in Victorian times. Nearby was a fragment of a Saxon cross and the Centurion Inn, marking the course of the Wall. Tall lime trees circled the heart of the village and bound the settlement together; without its trees, Walton would be much the poorer.

Green-veined white butterfly

By Sandysike Farm, and via a weir over the river Cam, a footpath led south-west to Newtown. House Wood hid the Irthing and the site of

Castlesteads Fort. Across the A6071 and along a side-road to Whiteflat, the ridge and furrow of the Wall and ditch was then easy enough to follow along field edges.

To the south is the wide level expanse of Carlisle Airport. During the Second World War this was a bomber base and more extensive than it is now. The local doctor at the time, Harry Nelson, tells of how the district nurses sometimes got lost trying to follow short-cuts back to the cottage hospital along unsigned, unlit tracks. The rural population of Brampton had been boosted at the time by a trainful of pregnant mothers from Tyneside, and at least two evacuees had their babies delivered somewhere in the wilderness of the Crosby aerodrome in the early hours of a morning.

Past Bleatarn Farm, over a shallow brow of pasture, the path met the end of a stony track and passed White Moss. Once, the whole area of Crosby Moor was a mosaic of heather and scrub, more like southern heathland than moorland. All that remains is the patch called White Moss, bounded by the Wall to the north and the Stanegate to the south. In Roman times there would have been more marshy ground and fewer trees, but the character of the Moss would have been much the same. The Vallum, about a hundred yards south of the track, was visible as ridges parallel to the track. It was built by heaping up banks rather than digging a ditch, so that the whole structure wouldn't sink into the mire.

Half way along the track lay a dead adder, a beautifully marked male half a metre long and probably about six years old. The track was only being used by farm machinery, busy with silage, but the snake had been run over and was probably killed in the morning, before he had warmed up enough to be able to get out of the way. His eyes were hard and bright as rubies.

A road continues the line of the Wall from Wall Head Farm to Walby, from where there were two possible ways forward. One ran south along Birky Lane ('birk' is an old name for birch) then crossed the B6234 and led through Linstock to Rickerby Park on the north bank of the Eden. This links up with the route for the National Trail and certainly looked peaceful. The alternative was to keep faith with the Wall and endure the suburbs of Carlisle and the traffic of the A69. This was the shorter and quicker option and towards the end of a long day it seemed the right
thing to do. In fact it was the right thing in every way, for there is more to Carlisle than meets the eye.

Male adder, from the track at White Moss.

The ditch of the Wall ran straight through Brunstock Park, next to the main road, and was full of rushes and sedges. Cattle were grazing up to the fence at its edge and reaching over to the tall canary grass and sedges. Eventually a pair of mallards lost their nerve and burst from beneath one of the cow's feet. The duck sprang first and was well into the air before the drake joined her. Together, but always with the duck ahead, they circled to the north, almost out of sight, then returned and dropped into the ditch only a hundred yards from where they had started. Nearby, lapwings picked at the cuffed ground where the cattle had been.

The B6264 crossed the M6 by the old pele of Drawdykes, overlooking the cutting where motorway traffic sped northwards through the ghost of the Wall. Further into town there were side-roads which offered glimpses of hedges and filled-in ditches, obviously following a theme, but after Tarraby, and the Near Boot Inn on the Vallum, there was nothing left to look for.

The day was nearly over, even with several hours' light still in the sky. Down Whitecross Gate, and past compact suburbs and the old college walls, Carlisle was drifting into evening and people were walking their dogs. There was no way of reconciling the secure atmosphere of this modern town with its razor-edge existence of younger years. It had been the most important settlement on the English side of the border. Even before the Wall was built there had been a Roman fort in Old Carlisle, on the south side of the Eden close to the present position of Tullie House. Soon after the Wall came Petriana, at Stanwix on this side of the river, the biggest fort on the frontier with a garrison of 1000 cavalry soldiers, the Ala Augusta Petriana. This was where the Ninth Legion came, and may be where they were destroyed (the fate of the vanished Ninth is one of the enduring mysteries of the occupation).

But turning left into the streets of Stanwix, on a high promontory overlooking the River Eden, there was nothing to see and no whispers of history.

A tired chill, the reward of a long day, crept into every limb.

7 Carlisle-Bowness

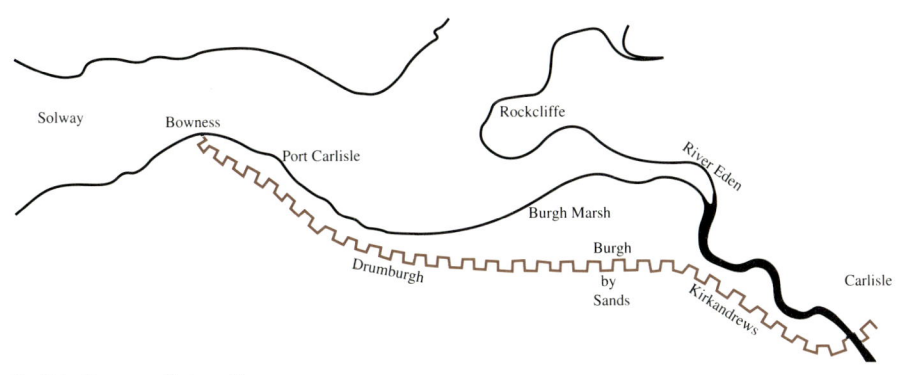

Carlisle-Bowness: 12 1/2 miles

The A7 into Carlisle is for cars in a hurry. It wasn't always so; even the new Eden Bridge, built in the nineteenth century, must have known quieter times. Yet the change was well under way by the turn of the century. When Maria Hoyer travelled the Wall in 1908 she stayed at Carlisle and fell into conversation with a party of tourists: *"They had come from Windermere that day. They seemed quite intelligent beings, but they supposed there was nothing to see in Carlisle... They went off next morning for Alnwick. Such are the ways of motorists. Their only care is to get themselves carried about like parcels as quickly as possible."* Easy to stand in judgement when you have thrown off the parcel wrappings for a few days and are measuring by Roman miles.

Early maps show two bridges on the Stanwix-Carlisle road, and it must have been one of these that figured in the retelling of the story of Christie's Willie in Sir Walter Scott's 'Border Minstrelsy'. Christie's Willie was the nickname of William Armstrong, a descendant of the infamous Armstrongs of Liddesdale. He had undertaken to act as messenger between Charles 1 and the Earl of Traqhair, but having stopped at Carlisle to refresh his horse he found the 'long, high, narrow bridge' held by Cromwell's forces. Undaunted, he spurred his horse over the parapet and into the river. Fortunately it was in spate and the water deep enough to break his fall.

Carried downstream some distance, he managed to scramble his horse ashore and made a dash for Scotland, pursued by troopers. Once across the Esk he knew he was safe and in true Armstrong fashion, turned and invited the troopers to join him in a drink. This may sound far-fetched, but the history of Carlisle is laced with swashbuckling adventures and dubious characters. *"Merrie Carlisle"*, wrote Robert Borland, *"where so many famous freebooters, at one time or other, have paid the last penalty of the law."*

Steps led down from the noisy road to the south bank of the Eden. Tall shrubs and giant clumps of Himalayan balsam and Japanese knotweed hid the path. Rivers have always been an easy highway for invaders: the seeds of these aliens must have found their way down every waterway in the country. They were introduced into Victorian gardens but soon made good their escape and now menace walkers with their heavy scent, exploding pods and dinner-plate leaves.

A few yards further on there were several kinds of native Umbellifers, the family of plants characterised by 'umbels' or crowded discs of tiny flowers on tall straight stems. The umbels are intended as landing platforms for pollinating insects such as wasps and hover-flies. Although Umbellifers look more appropriate to the British landscape, and include such edible species as carrot and angelica, they also include very poisonous plants such as water dropwort and hemlock, the source of the classic root-brew used to dispatch the Greek philosopher Socrates. It pays to know your umbels.

Hemlock is easily identified by its crimson-speckled stem; there was none by the Eden bridge and all the umbellifers were innocent. It was too early for the hogweed to be out, but the furled buds were opening and last year's dried skeletons were still in place, bearing clusters of seeds bound by cobwebs. The crushed seeds gave off a refreshing orange-peel scent. Cow parsley was in full flower, lining the upper bank with shivering lace leaves and a mist of cream-coloured flower-heads, and there were a few clumps of the more robust sweet cicely. The climate of northern England must suit sweet cicely, for it grows better here than anywhere. Its leaves and seeds give off a pungent scent of aniseed, just like fennel, so that the smell of either plant can conjure an image of byways in Durham or Provence.

A path to the left led away from the river to Carlisle Castle. This and Tullie House warrant a day to themselves, for although the city of Carlisle may have succumbed in some ways to mediocrity and the motor car, the castle has escaped and Tullie House contains some fine displays of the city's glorious days. So whilst keeping to the river it was impossible not to look left.

Carlisle Castle hardly fits the romantic notion of a mediaeval fortress, but with castles it is more important to tell a good story than to look pretty. The keep was built on the orders of William Rufus in 1092, and shortly after this a curtain wall was added. Thus endowed it became the prize in many a war between English and Scottish kings, assaulted by William the Lion and captured (briefly) by Alexander II. In 1283 Edward I made Robert Bruce its custodian, but after a few years he had the bruising Scot replaced by the Bishop of Carlisle, in whose care it was extensively repaired. Edward used the castle quite often, assembling parliament here in 1306 and planning campaigns. It was repaired in the reign of Edward III and again in the reign of Edward IV, under the governorship of the Duke of Gloucester (later Richard III). Henry VIII had the whole castle fortified with artillery, and in 1568 Mary Queen of Scots was held here.

After the Civil War, when the castle changed hands several times, Carlisle settled back in the knowledge that the border conflicts were past and there was no longer any strategic value in the place. This peaceful affluence lasted until 1745. Nobody took Prince Charles Edward Stuart seriously, and it must have come as a nasty surprise when he slipped John Cope's army and camped outside Carlisle Castle on 9th of November 1745. On the 15th of November the castle surrendered and the whole country held its breath.

Bonnie Prince Charlie marched south as far as Derby, but his army then retreated back to Scotland and the rebellion was soon over. Afterwards there were serious questions to be answered. Lt Col James Durant was singled out as the scapegoat and at his court martial he issued a statement in mitigation: *"The Militia... having absolutely to a man refused to defend the castle, and the Garrison, consisting only of two companies of invalids amounting to about eighty men... and the castle very large, so that there are neither men to manage the guns nor man the walls, and the mayor and the inhabitants of the town, together with the officers of the Militia, having sent to treat with the rebels... and being refused any terms... the castle not being tenable, it is for his majesty's service that it be abandoned"*. Poor Durant must have thought even this insufficient an excuse for he then went on to explain that he had been suffering from gout when the siege took place. He was found innocent, having wisely implicated the whole city in the surrender.

The Roman bridge and Wall crossed the Eden at a cusp in the S bend around Stanwix, from what is now the sports field to a point just upstream of the confluence of the river Caldew. Camden noticed 'mighty stones' in the main channel in the 16th century, and dredging work in 1951 proved the point by uncovering dozens more sandstone blocks. Nothing is now visible, and on an overcast morning it was impossible to see into the turbid waters. A common tern, buoyant as thistle-down, hovered close to the mouth of the Caldew but saw no fish and moved back downstream. Across the footbridge and following the path beside the Eden, Sheepmount Playing Field and the main railway line lay to the left, partly screening the dereliction of the city's industry. No trains passed; the heyday of steam has been consigned to history along with the Romans and the reivers. A line of willows and poplars followed the curve of the river and from the lower branches of a willow, without any obvious nesting thicket in sight, a whitethroat burst into song.

Tail-feather of green woodpecker.

Beneath the railway bridge and away from the plain of Sheepmount, waste tips and sewage works soured the air and made it difficult to believe that less than an hour's walk away lay one of the best wildlife sites in the north, and that one of the prettiest butterflies, the marsh fritillary, would be on the wing. It took discipline to stay with the Eden at its least lovely, to the edge of the city where pylons spanned the broadening river and sand martins and swallows hawked for gnats with a persistence borne of hunger. One path followed the river, below a wall of trees screening the steep bluff of Davidson's Banks. Hadrian's Wall once stood atop the bank and the trees gave a good impression of the way it would have dominated the outlook to the north. Another path followed the field edge at the top of the bank and offered a more varied route.

Past the pylons at Knockupworth, and the gill or stream that marks the city boundary, the landscape threw off its tired mantle and turned green again. No stones of the Wall were left standing between here and Bowness but there were ample patterns in the earth to keep the thread going.

The Vallum was very clear in the pastures a few yards to the south of Davidson's Banks and it was possible to make out gaps in the north mound where the peaceful phase of Roman occupation resulted in the cutting of wagonways. On the deeper soil, among drifts of taller grass, there were wild flowers such as germander speedwell, birds' foot trefoil, greater stitchwort and tufted vetch. The pebble-dash of colours - blue, yellow, white and purple - attracted little *Andrena* bees which were digging their nest-burrows in the earth walls of sheep-scrapes in the berm and mound of the Vallum.

A much more obvious earthwork across the fields and away to the north-west was the cutting created in the 1820s for a canal and used subsequently for a railway line.

Neither was successful, and the only moment of glory for the canal was when it was used by a barge carrying Stephenson's Rocket down to Liverpool.

Thickets of blackthorn and hawthorn and stands of oak, ash and elm continued northwards along the high bank of the river and made navigation easy, even when the path disappeared into fields of potatoes and the Vallum struck out on its own to the north-west. The enclosure hedges were all hawthorn, the 'quickthorn' planted by the million in the late eighteenth and early nineteenth centuries to parcel up the land and create what we now think of as timeless Albion.

Four Suffolk tups sat shoulder to shoulder in the hollow beneath one of the hedges. They had been clipped and looked rather foolish, but put on belligerent expressions. One of them, with a bald grey face rather than the usual black, shook its head so that its ears clacked together.

The remaining May blossom on the hedges was browned at the edges and there were already some nests of small ermine moth caterpillars woven around the axils of the branches. There are several species of small ermine, all similar in appearance (silver with black dots) but with quite different foodplants. The one that attacks hawthorn is called *Yponomeuta padella.* Because of their communal habits, which result in the defoliation of bushes, the silk webs and nests of caterpillars are noticed by everyone, but the pretty little adult moths pass unseen. A stand of bird cherry, sallow or hawthorn that has been infested by small ermines looks quite ghostly. Fortunately the bushes have evolved a strategy to cope with the annual disaster; when the caterpillars have stripped the first flush of foliage and pupated the bushes are able to send out a fresh set of leaves which lasts through the summer.

Wild cherry growing in the hedgerow.

The Eden made another loop, arching eastwards to seek out the easiest but longest route to the Solway. The meanders were getting broader all the time. At this point the Wall also struck off westwards; either the Romans grew weary of the river as a defence or its course has changed. Rivers are alive, feeding and growing and writhing as they shift their ground, but the pace of their movement is so much slower than our own that we are usually unable to detect it.

The little village of Grinsdale clustered around two farms. From the road a track led off opposite Eden Holme and through Park Farm, then picked up the obvious line of the Wall on the crest of the hill. On either side of the flailed hawthorn hedge there were fields of bright green grass, cut for silage and looking so sappy that the nitrogen almost glowed. A huge tractor scorched up the track, bouncing off the ruts as it went and scaring the gang of rooks that had been digging for worms on the cut ground. Inside the tractor-cab sat a big man, wearing an expression like the Suffolk tups and clearly not inclined to pass the time of day.

Climbing the pasture on the far side of Sourmilk Bridge, where the little Doudle Beck was crossed at the site of a Wall turret, the missing Wall followed the crest of a ridge, with a view east to the meander of the Eden.

The Wall ran along the top of the South bank of the Eden.

It becomes possible, with familiarity, to predict the line of the Wall, simply by bearing engineering requirements in mind and remembering that the legions were facing north, looking for the clearest advantage in the lie of the land.

Kirkandrews, the next village, was prosperous and quiet. Wisteria-draped houses slept in the shadows. Past Eden Farm there was a tiny graveyard, hedged and edged by tall limes and entered by a creaking iron gate. The headstones, of weathered sandstone dabbed by lichens, stood in a waving sea of vernal grass. There is no church left to give the place its meaning, but it was more peaceful for the absence. Just past what must have been the rectory was a path to the right which led back to the bank above the Eden. The river was on the cusp of another curve, eroding the west bank and depositing silt for future farmland on the east. The steep woodland backed onto some elegant houses and the path squeezed between their gardens and the falling ground. A young couple were out cutting down an adolescent sycamore on the upper slope of the woodland, trying to open up a patch of ground to create what they called a Wild Garden. Whether the other sycamores would allow this to happen is doubtful.

The river almost vanished from sight down to the right, hidden by dense foliage. It was a beautiful, ancient fragment of 'wildwood' and the flora reflected this; springs made the ground moist and there were big patches of bluebell, campion, butterbur and water avens. There was also a clump of giant hogweed, an alien Umbellifer of mammoth proportions, capable of growing ten feet tall in a few days. Local authorities have been trying to eradicate it, not because of its size but because people brushing past the plant are liable to come out in a painful rash; the hairs that cover the plant contain a chemical which reacts with Vitamin D, so people out on sunny days are at the greatest risk.

After a few hundred yards the path led out onto a road and the Eden was finally lost. It was noon on a bright but cloudy day. Farm buildings along the road into Beaumont were made busy with nesting swallows, which were hunting over the river but circling back and rushing headlong through an old damson orchard on their approach to the barns and byres.

Beaumont lay on a knoll, hence the name. The houses were gathered around a green and the settlement had a feudal atmosphere, but its origins went back much further and the grassy mound on which the little church sits is on the line of the Wall. The mound was a motte, the site of a small but significant castle and the home of the le Brun family, in the days when everybody who was anybody had friends and relations in Normandy. Eventually the le Bruns became the de la Ferte's. According to Hodgson this name was a reflection on the kind of land in the family's ownership, mainly to the west: *"In antient times, the middle part of the parish was so full of peat bogs and marshes as to have acquired the name of Feritas, or the Wilderness: and the le Brun family, its proprietors, De Feritate."* There are still bogs and marshes towards Bowness, but no longer any families with the proprietorial name of Bogman.

The church stood high and proud, within a cordon of pollarded limes and a wall embanking the grassy dome. The headstones of the graves were awash in a green sea, but this time enlivened by the translucent yellow flowers of hawkweed.

Leaving the church by the south gate the road to Kirkandrews lay ahead. A few yards from the corner, and worth the short detour, the wall bore a Roman stone, built into its fabric and almost worn away. Presumably this was what Bruce described as part of a building stone of the fifth cohort of the Twentieth Legion. It was impossible to make any sense of what remained of the carving. It was difficult to know what to feel about finding it in such a state. Some of the raised markings had been scraped by a lorry or bus and were freshly chipped or smeared in blue paint. Perhaps the stone should have been in a museum, or protected in some way. But having seen so many inscribed stones in dreary displays it was good to see one in the landscape, a palpable link with the men who carved it, open to the elements and destined to turn to dust.

A lane led from Beaumont through fields westwards towards Burgh. When it came to an end the ghost of the Wall carried on. North of Wormanby Farm there was a footbridge over the Powburgh Beck, and a little way upstream there were scattered stones which may have been the point where the Military way, the Roman access road, crossed the stream. There was even a wooden post jutting out of the bank beneath the water, looking just as stained and weathered as it should. It was much too good to be true. Further on, past Spillblood Holm and the place where Hangman Tree once stood, and past the levelled site of a medieval castle, lay Burgh by Sands.

About a mile north of the village is Burgh Marsh, which marks where the Eden ends and the Solway estuary begins. Burgh Marsh lies on the south side of the river-mouth and Rockcliffe Marsh lies to the north. In the early winter, before the close of the shooting season, these marshes are home to thousands of barnacle geese. In the late winter they move down the estuary to Caerlaverock and in the spring they migrate back to their breeding grounds on Spitzbergen. The Solway plays host to the entire population. The attraction for the geese, and for the summer-nesting lapwings and redshank, is the grass. Mile upon mile of dense turf, mostly composed of red fescue and saltmarsh grass, stretches across the head of the Solway.

During the summer Burgh Marsh is grazed by a motley assortment of sheep and cattle, which keep the turf cropped and fertilized. The result is the best grass available in Europe, and there is a steady trade in dispatching it to such places as Wimbledon.

The Solway tides are notorious. Over the years the sea-level has dropped but this has only made the marshes more dangerous; creeks are narrow and deep and the tide rushes through them quicker than a person can run. The Burgh Marshes are being eroded and undercut, whilst the Rockcliffe Marshes are actually growing. Crossing the Solway is a risky business, but it can be done by those who know the tides and channels. Hence the Roman's need for the Wall to go all the way to Bowness.

In the summer of 1307, Edward I was camped out on the Burgh Marsh waiting for the right opportunity to take an army into Scotland. By then he was a sick man; he died in his tent and the final victory, his life's ambition, was denied him. *"Thus"*, in the words of the Chronicle of Lanercost, *"Edward the younger succeeded the elder, but in the same manner as Rehoboam succeeded Soloman"*. This was written only a few years after the event and was a dangerous thing to say; it must have been obvious already that Edward II was not going to make an 'illustrious and excellent king'. What lay ahead was centuries of bitter struggle between the two rising nations.

A monument was erected where Edward died, built out of Wall stone by the Duke of Norfolk in 1685. It fell down a century later and was rebuilt in its present elaborate form by the Earl of Lonsdale, whose descendant now leases the Marsh to the National Trust. The monument is visible for miles around, but it is an ugly thing.

Burgh, pronounced Bruff, is a neat linear village, built out of stone from the Roman fort of Aballava. The Wall met the fort towards the eastern edge of the present settlement. Having seen nothing but ghosts over the last few miles it was a surprise to be faced with something tangible.

From the grassy cemetery, raised several feet above the adjacent field, it was possible to visualise the fort; otherwise the stones, and particularly those of St Michael's Church, whispered secrets that were too garbled to understand.

St Michael's was built in the early twelfth century and altered, or rebuilt, in the thirteenth century. Edward I was brought to the spot after his death on 7th July 1307. Border wars soon forced more alterations and a fortified tower was added in the fourteenth century. This was the west tower, built by and for the villagers. There was an east tower too, the vicar's house, but that fell down centuries ago. From the outside the west tower looked solid. Arrow slits were its only eyes, and there was no door at all. The only entrance was from within the church, where there was a small square doorway in the nave. It looked pitch black inside, and the heavy iron

Dog Rose

gate or yett looked as if it might be locked, but shoulder pressure swung it open and it was then possible to step inside. What had seemed imposing from the outside suddenly diminished to something the size of a box room. It was cold and damp and the tiny windows, made even smaller by the massive thickness of the walls, barely pierced the gloom. There was a grim atmosphere. What must it have been like to huddle here when a raid was on, to know that your home was being put to the torch, your friends or family killed and your cattle driven away? They were bitter times.

Hunter Davies looked round the church twenty years ago, and the vicar at the time, Jack Strong, showed him some pottery dug up from the old rectory garden and pointed out some carvings. The garden has now made way for a new house, but the carvings were easy to find inside the church. The most interesting and enigmatic of these were a pagan head to the left of the altar and a pair of mythical beasts in the lintel of the west tower door.

Spillblood Holm, east of Burgh by Sands. The line of the Wall is picked out by the hedge lines and trees.

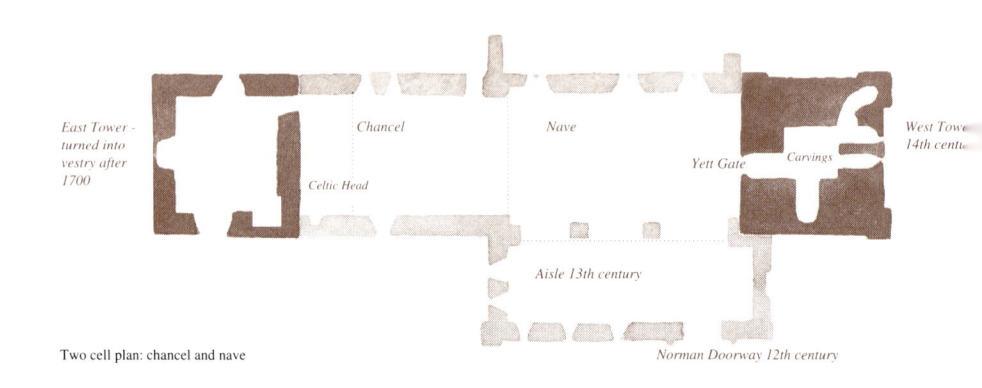

East Tower - turned into vestry after 1700

Chancel

Celtic Head

Nave

Yett Gate

Carvings

West Tower 14th century

Aisle 13th century

Norman Doorway 12th century

Two cell plan: chancel and nave

Plan of St Michael's Church.
The thick walls of the West Tower are a clue to its ulterior use as a defensive stronghold.

St Michael's Church, Burgh-by-Sands.
The church and churchyard lie within the Roman fort of Aballaua.

Celtic carvings on the lintel of the west tower of St Michael's Church, Burgh.

Pagan head to the left of the altar.

The carvings were impressive and must have meant something very special to the people who created them. The Church Warden thought the head came to light during eighteenth century excavation work for the chancel floor. Mr Strong described them as 'Moorish' in style, because the Roman fort was garrisoned by Aurelian Moors, but the latest theories, according to the new vicar's wife, are that both the head and the beasts are of Celtic design.

Beyond Burgh and its outlying hamlet of Dykesfield the Vallum and the line of the Wall disappear into Burgh Marsh, which has obviously eaten into the farmland as the channel of the Eden has swung

Wood Avens

south. The whole character of the walk changed in an instant; the sky opened, the ground levelled and the views broadened. An onshore breeze set the thrift flowers dancing in pink waves across the marsh. Cattle and sheep grazed as far as the eye could see and Scotland was in sight.

The road shadowed the dyke of the old railway and canal; the landscape had such a strong flavour of the Fens that it was easy to imagine a drain or fields of sugar beet and wheat on the other side of the dyke. Drumburgh dispelled the illusion by being very Cumbrian, a mix of old farms and modern bungalows on a knoll surrounded by pasture. The ghost of the Wall climbed back out of the marsh to the top of the knoll where there had been a fort, Congavata, once garrisoned by a vexillation of the Second Cohort of Lingones. The view from the field behind the modern houses was astonishingly good, especially of the estuary to the north.

Most of the stone from the little fort went to build Drumburgh Castle, a manor-house with farm attached, a few yards down the road to the east. A Roman altar stood against the wall on the west side, inviting a closer look, but although there was a shuffling sound from somewhere inside, no-one answered the door.

The le Brun family, much closer now to the wilderness, built the first fortified house here in 1307 but this was ruinous by the sixteenth century when Lord Dacre had this 'pretty pyle' erected out of the residue.

Two megalithic birds, with stumpy wings outstretched, perched on the eaves high above the main door. It was mid-afternoon and time to move on.

The mark of the Wall was clear to see in the sweep of pasture between Drumburgh and Glasson. Away to the left lay Glasson Moss and Bowness Common; the Romans had avoided what must then have been a hopeless sweep of heaths and mires and had kept close to the coast. In 1903 a peat-digger discovered 'ancient palisadings' of wooden posts driven a foot into the underlying sand. The posts were two feet high and their tops were five feet below the surface of the bog, suggesting that peat-formation, and the growth of the Sphagnum bog, had been rapid. Today a lot of the wilderness has been drained, but a lot still remains. The Bowness-Kirkbride road separates the two main areas, of which Glasson Moss is smaller and less spoilt by burning, drainage or digging. Like all bogs its greatest beauty is its treasure of flowers, including sweet gale, bog rosemary and all three kinds of sundew.

Altar stone above door

Only two miles, even less in the Roman equivalent, remained of the route to Maia, the last fort along the Wall. The site of the 78th milecastle was mid-way between Glasson and Port Carlisle and a short stones-throw

from the spring tide-line. Unfortunately the sea was out for the day.
Westfield Marsh was deserted except for a pair of shelducks and a barnacle goose. The goose was obviously a 'pricked' bird, shot and winged the previous winter and unable to leave with the rest of the flock. It had attached itself to the most goose-like creatures it could find, but the drake shelduck was not sympathetic and was dividing its time between displaying to its mate and threatening the goose. Shelducks are aggressive by nature and the poor goose was torn between wanting to be close to its new family and having to keep its distance.

The green sward of the marsh was pitted and crazed by a network of dry creeks, a few inches wide but several feet deep. From their glistening depths came rich oozing noises and the smell of salt and sulphur. Beyond the lip of the marsh was a lower shelf of seablite, thrift and scurvy-grass, then the inter-tidal mudflats. Eastriggs and Gretna lay three or four miles away on the far side of the estuary.

In winter the mud and sand of the Solway is washed clean almost every day, but in the summer it looks grimy and forgotten by the tide. By Kirkland Scar stands Port Carlisle, the terminus for the failed canal and railway line. An elaborate harbour was built here with the intention of making this Carlisle's gateway to the world. What remains has been reshaped by the sea into a narrow island and buttresses of sandstone blocks, and a series of oak beams and breakers like the ribs of a half-buried whale.

Haaf nets, the oblong framed nets used for catching salmon in the Solway shallows, stood propped up against banks of tamarisk waiting for the tide. At the north end of the village, on the left side of the road, stood Hesket House, referred to in literature as the Steam Packet Hotel and famous because of the Roman altar stone built into the lintel. It was clear enough to see but surprisingly small and the lower words were missing. 'MATRI BVSSVIS' remained, the usual kind of obscure shorthand by which soldiers acknowledged their gods. The line of the Wall crossed the road a few yards further on, turning west through the end terrace and out across the flat pasture. The nine-foot wide foundations lie just below the surface, straight to the site of the last milecastle, then north-west into Bowness. In Hadrian's day Bowness was more of a cape; the sea curled around its eastern side and the tide almost lapped the footings of the Wall. Clearly, these fields were not here then. The Wall itself would have been made of turf, which may have caused some concern among the auxiliaries who manned it in times of storm.

Being in sight of Bowness it seemed perverse not to follow the lay-line of the Wall, but this is impossible because there was no footpath. The only way of making all-important contact with the last mile of its course was to cut across the fields a few hundred yards further along the road. Although there are various references to 'massive fragments' of the Wall still standing in this area there was nothing there. However, having come so far this didn't seem to matter. Unfortunately a deep drain barred the final few yards and the only comfortable way of entering the village was past Grey Havens, along the road or the shore.

By now the sea was a distant line in the main channel of the estuary, flowing over the last fordable point of Bowness Wath. In the spring,

The end of the Wall at Bowness. Nothing is visible, but stonework lies buried in the foreground, on the banks of the Solway.

seabirds such as kittiwakes and skuas gain altitude here before crossing to the Firth of Forth on their northern migration, and in the autumn the organic mix of mud and sand along the beach attracts wading birds such as little stints and curlew sandpipers. But early summer is not the time to expect anything so interesting; gulls and crows had taken over the tide-line and were picking over the flotsam in search of sand-hoppers or carrion.

It was early evening in Bowness. There were no cars on the main street and all was quiet. Having three hours daylight and nowhere to go was an unexpected luxury. All that remained was to seek out any traces of the Wall's end and the fort of Maia, then look to the setting sun and turn for home. Maia had been a big fort of eight acres. The site was perfectly chosen, though the Romans probably replaced a settlement that was already there, alongside the ancient mound known as the Rampire. The present village has spread out to cover the area of the fort but has then grown parallel with the coast rather than inland, which is where the vicus or civilian settlement had been. Walking along the tideline, past more haaf nets, the village looked as if it had been built on a dome of soil and rubble which was sliding away on the seaward side. Hodgson described the material more elaborately as *"stiff reddish clay, embedded with diluvial blocks of granite grauwacce... and other primary and tertiary rocks"* : rubble by any other name, but dumped by nature.

The hidden line of the Wall approaches the cape of Bowness by turning west on the east edge of the village, crossing the road just beyond some new houses ('Curlews' and 'Coxwold') and behind a black-and-white painted terrace. Apart from the name 'Hadrian Cottage', on the building under which the Wall passed, there was no concession to history in the whole village; no signs or notices, no shops selling leaflets, not a word of interpretation. The only visible artifact, apart from all the re-used stone, was an altar, found in a nearby field in 1739 and embedded into a barn wall. Books describe it as an inscribed altar to Jupiter, and the more recent texts say it was 'damaged'. In fact there was nothing left on it at all except for a few ripple marks in the rotting sandstone. An old man leaning on the gate opposite said he could remember there being some writing on it, but not for twenty years. As at Beaumont it was sad to see the inscription lost for ever, but not as sad as seeing it 'conserved', either in situ or in a museum. Reading the inscription from a book, 'IOM PRO SALVTE DD NN : GALLI ET VOLVSIANI AVGG SVLPICIUS : SECVNDIAN VS TRIB COH POSVIT', and looking at the blank face of stone, was like witnessing Shelley's Osymandias; 'Look on my works, ye Mighty, and despair!'

Families were returning from a fete on the school field at the far end of the village; music played and buntings brightened the roadside. Just beyond the school, where the raised plateau of Maia dropped to the shore and the ghost of the Wall was extinguished, it was at last possible to look out to the open sea. A flock of curlews banked and landed on the sands having flighted out from Bowness Common. Oystercatchers slept in twos and threes, waiting for the tide. A barn owl, mobbed by crows, rose from its roost among the bushes of the old railway viaduct and drifted into the evening shadows.

Small stone altar above a barn door in Bowness.
The words have been washed away over the last few years.

Waders on the Solway.

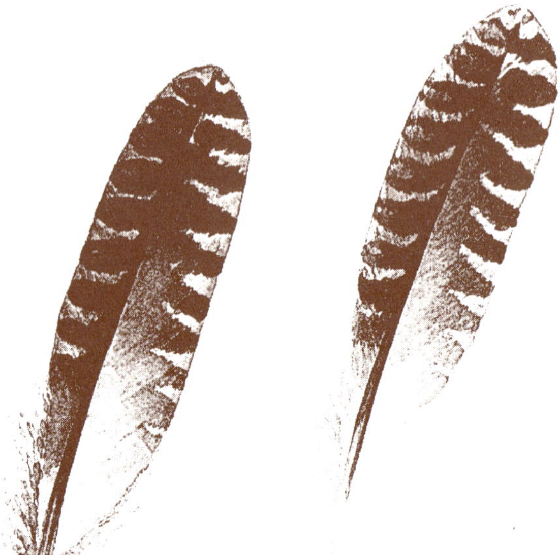

Further Information

This book is a personal interpretation of the Wall and is not intended as a user guide. To plan your own walk, or to follow up any snippets of information, there are several guidebooks covering the Roman sites. These include an English Heritage guide, and a series of useful booklets produced about individual sites such as Vindolanda. The two classic textbooks about Hadrian's Wall are by Breeze and Dobson and Collingwood Bruce; the latter was first published in 1863 but has been updated and is still the best handbook in print. Hunter Davis' *Walk Along The Wall* is certainly the best anecdotal story about Hadrian's Wall, but a facsimile of William Hutton's walk in 1801 is available as a Frank Graham booklet and is a delightful antidote to the heavier guides. Information about non-Roman things is scanty. Northumberland National Park has produced an educational field guide, which covers general aspects of land use and ecology as well as history, and *Hadrian's Birds* by Miles and Henry covers bird-watching and habitats.

For specific information, the following organisations may be able to help:
English Heritage,
Arnhem Block, The Castle, Carlisle, Cumbria CA3 8UR
Cumbria Tourist Board,
Ashleigh, Holly Road, Windermere, Cumbria LA23 2AQ
National Trust,
Scot's Gap, Morpeth, Northumberland NE61 4EG
Northumberland National Park,
Eastburn, South Park, Hexham, Northumberland NE46 1BS
Northumbria Tourist Board,
Aykley Heads, Durham DH1 5UX

The next best thing to going out and exploring the Wall is to visit one of the museums or visitor centres. The best are those at Tullie House in Carlisle, Vindolanda near Bardon Mill and the Museum of Antiquities at the University of Newcastle. Others worth a visit along the way are those at Corstopitum, Chesters, Housesteads, Once Brewed and Birdoswald.

When walking the Wall, remember to keep to the rights of way or ask permission from land-owners, and take special care when walking along the Military Road; cars travel fast and there is no side-walk.

Some of the locations and wildlife sites described in this book have been disguised to prevent possible disturbances.

INDEX

Aballava 130
Aesica 90-94
Agricola 2, 36, 43, 55, 111
Alkali Inn 8
Alum House Inn 7
Andromeda 71
Antimony Works 14
Arbeia 5-6
Armstrong, Ralph 9
Armstrong, William 121
Asphodel 71

Badger 73
Baltic Flour Mill 18
Banks 112
Banks East 111
Banna 110
Barbarian Conspiracy 102
Barcombe Fell 72
Barn owl 102-103, 140
Barnacle goose 130
Bass Rock 4
Beaumont 128, 129
Bede, Venerable 9, 12, 36
Benedict Biscop 9
Bewick, Thomas 22
Birdoswald 102, 108
Bishop's House 31
Black Carts 62
Black Dyke 68, 69
Black rat 27
Blackface sheep 79
Blackfriars 20
Blenkinsop Common 101
Bonnie Prince Charlie 123-124
Border Leicester 79
Bowness 138-139
Bowness Wath 138
Bradley Green 83
Brocolitia 64-67
Brown hare 41
Brown rat 27

Bruce, Collingwood 20- 22, 27
Bruce, Robert 123
Brunstock Park 119
Brunton Turret 53
Burgh Marsh 129, 130, 135
Burgh-by-Sands 129, 131-135
Business Park 27
Byker Wall 16
Byker Bridge 17

Cadwallon 50
Carlisle 118-119, 121-124
Carlisle Castle 123
Carr Hill 45
Carrawbrough 64
Carvoran 99,102
Castle Garth 23
Castle Nick 86
Castlesteads Fort 118
Cawfields Crags 89
Cheviot sheep 79
Chronicle of Lanercost 130
Cilurnum 60-62
Chollerford Bridge 53, 54, 59, 60
Chesters Fort 54, 60-62
Clayton, John 54, 60, 62
Cockmount Hill 94
Coelfrith, Abbot 12
Cowyn's Cross 77-78
Congavata 135
Cookson, Catherine 8
Cooperage, the 25
Copthorne Hotel 25
Corporation Quay 7
Corstopitum 43
Coulson,
John Blenkinsop 101-102
Coventina's Well 66
Cow parsley 123
Craggle Hill 112, 114
Cranberry 71
Curlew 41, 64

INDEX

Curlew Road 14
Danom 14
Davidson's Banks 125
Davis, Hunter 131
Denton 28-31
Denton Dene 28
Denton Hall 30
Dere Street 43, 45, 47
Dipper 57
Dolerite 63, 89
Don, River 9, 13
Down Hill 46
Downy birch 84
Drumburgh 135
Drumburgh Castle 135
Durant, Lt Col James 124
Durham Tower 21
Dutch Elm Disease 35, 51

East Jarrow 8, 14
Ecgfrith, King 12
Eden, River 120, 122, 124, 127, 128
Edward I 83-84, 99, 113, 123, 130, 131
Edward II 130
Edwin 50
Ever Tower 19

Fossway 16
Fox 87-88

Gannet 1, 4
Giant hogweed 128
Gilsland 102, 104
Glasson Moss 136
Goosander 59
Gorse 48
Graving Dock 7
Great Chesters 90-94
Great North Reservoir 39
Greathead, Henry 5

Green-veined white butterfly 117
Greenhead 101
Grindon Lough 68, 70
Grinsdale 127
Groyne Lighthouse 3
Guildhall 24-25

Haltonchesters 46
Hadrian Road 15
Hadrian Yard 15
Hare Hill 114
Harlow Hill 39
Harrison, David 45-46
Haughton Common 68, 76
Hawk Side 68, 78
Hawthorn 62, 126
Heber Tower 19
Heddon-on-the-Wall 38
Hefenfelt 50
Hemlock 122, 123
High Level Bridge 22
High Shield Crags 85
Hill Head Farm 49
Himalayan balsam 122
Housesteads 74-75
Hoyer, Maria 66, 121
Hutton, William 36, 39, 52, 55, 72, 87, 97
Horsley, John 67

Irthinghead mires 104
Irthing, River 102, 103-107

Japanese knotweed 122
Jarrow 8-14
Jarrow Slake 8-9, 13
Jobling, William 9

Keelman's Hospital 17
Kirkandrews 128, 129
Kittiwake 1, 18, 138

INDEX

Lanercost Priory 112, 113-114
Large heath butterfly 72
Lawe 5
Lawe Top 2
le Brun family 129, 136
Leas 4
Lesser swallow prominent (moth) 53
Limestone Bank 63
Linnet 48
Littlehaven Beach 2-3

Maia 139,140
Maiden's Walk 27-28
Maison Dieu 24-25
Mare and Foal 89
Marsden 1
Marsden Rattler 4
Merlin 94-95
Military Road 44
Mithraic Temple 66
Montague, Lady 30
Morden Tower 19
Morwood 72
Muckle Moss 70

Nelson, Harry 118
Nether Denton Farm 111
Newburn 34

Newburn Country Park 35
Newcastle 2, 18, 19-31
Nine Nicks of Thirlwall 95, 108
North British Railway 54
North Tyne 56, 59
Northumberland
Wildlife Trust 70

Once Brewed (Youth Hostel & Visitor Centre) 87
Onnum 46-47
Osvald 50
Otter 56, 57
Oxford ragwort 6, 25
Oystercatcher 13, 41, 140

Palmate newt 64
Palmer Yard 13
Paradise 27-28
Peel Gap 86
Penda 50
Percy Pit 32
Peregrine 107
Petriana 120
Pike Hill 111
Planetrees Farm 51
Planetrees Field 52
Poltross Burn 102, 107
Pons Aelius 23
Port Carlisle 137
Portgate 47
Primrose 58
Puss moth 12-13
Rapishaw Gap 81
Red-necked grebe 76
Red squirrel 53-54, 70
Redshank 13-14
Redstart 106
Reid, John 8
Rendel, Daphne 24
Rock-rose 89
Roe deer 78
Rudchester 39
Rufus, William 123
Ryton Willows 34

St Andrew's Church 71
St Catherine's Hospital 25
St John's Church 21-22
St Mary's Church 117
St Michael's Church 131
St Nicholas' Cathedral 22
St Paul's Church 9-11
St Peter's Church 9
Samian Ware 66
Sandgate 18
Sandhill 23, 24
Scotswood Bridge 28
Scotswood Road 27, 28
Sea Road 4

INDEX

Seehaven Beach 4
Segedunum 15-16
Severus 6, 36, 55
Sewingshields 68, 69
Sewingshields Crag 76
Sheepmount 124, 125
Shieldsman ferry 7
Small ermine moth 126
Solway 129, 130, 137
South Shields 2-8
Sparrow-hawk 47, 73
Sphagnum 70
Spotted flycatcher 106
Stagshaw 47, 48
Stanegate 43, 70
Stanwix 120
Stella Power Station 34
Stephenson, George 15
Stowell Street 19, 21
Strong, Jack 131
Stukeley, Reverend 50
Sugley Dene 32
Swan Hunter 5, 15
Sweet cicely 123
Swing Bridge 23, 24
Sycamore Gap 85

Thirlwall 100
Thirlwall Castle 99
Town Walls 18, 19-31
Tulip, Henry 52
Tullie House 120, 123
Turf Wall 109, 111
Turner, William 84
Twice Brewed (Inn) 87

Tyne Docks 8
Tyne, River 3, 18, 22, 24
Tyne Tunnel 14

Vercovicium 75
Vickers Armstrong 28
Vindolanda 73
Vindovala 39

Wade, General 43, 50
Wall brown butterfly 14
Walwick 62
Warden Hill 53, 62
Westgate Road 21
West Walls, 19-31
Wallsend 16
Walltown 96-97
Walltown Crags 98
Walltown Quarry 98
Walton 117
Wapping Street 6-7
Westfield Marsh 137
Willowford 108
Wheatear 82
Whin Sill 63, 79
Whinshields 86
White Moss 118
Whittle Dene Reservoirs 39, 44
Wild chive 98
Willow warbler 3
Wood anemone 58
Wood cranesbill 58
Woodcock 95
Wouldhave, William 5

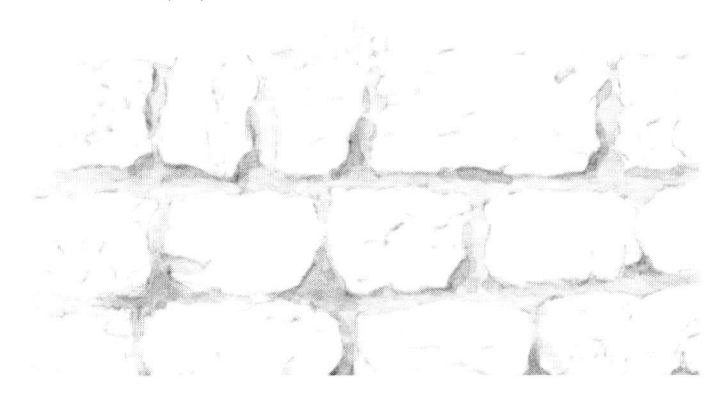